Good lu
in the
elk woods ☺

Best
wishes,

Jim Zumbo
Cody, WY
7-27-91

To Heck With Elk Hunting

By
Jim Zumbo

All photos by the author

Illustrated by Boots Reynolds

Dedication

To every experienced elk hunter, soon-to-be-an-elk- hunter
and maybe-some-day-will-be-an-elk-hunter –
may there be a big bull at the end of all your hunts,
and if there's not, enjoy the hunt for what it is,
rather than what it can produce for you.

ISBN: 0-9624025-2-4

Published by:
Jim Zumbo
Wapiti Valley Publishing Company
Box 2390
Cody, WY 82414

Publishing Consultant:

Jeri D. Walton
Outlaw Books Publishing
Box 4466, Bozeman, MT 59772

TABLE OF CONTENTS

INTRODUCTION

Hunting often has its bright sides — times when you can laugh at yourself and see humor in everyday situations. And that's the way it should be. We shouldn't ever take the sport so seriously that we can't have fun while participating. Camaraderie (a big word for fellowship) indeed has its place in hunting.

When I think back on my hunts, quite often those funny moments come to mind, but there were serious and awkward moments, too, many of which are recounted in this book.

To be sure, the hunter must stalk his quarry with seriousness, for a humane kill must be every hunter's objective. There's also time for reflection and emotions when we are fortunate enough to take an animal. But there will be those times when we'll find ourselves laughing. Humor is where you see it, and it's often spontaneous.

This book is quite different than my other two elk hunting books. Those works, HUNT ELK, and CALLING ALL ELK, are intended to instruct, inform, and educate readers to the ways of elk and proper hunting techniques.

As you'll see, TO HECK WITH ELK HUNTING is a collection of many of my hunts. I've tried to capture the human element — the spirit of the hunts as they unfolded. Whenever possible, I've highlighted the humorous aspects, some silly, some outrageous, and some almost unbelievable. Some of the chapters detail painful learning experiences, and are not at all humorous.

I've tried something else, too. As I wrote these tales, all of which are 100 percent true (honest), I injected many of the mistakes I've made, as well as some of the successes. I've bared my soul in some chapters, publicizing some incidents that have heretofore gone untold, such as my first elk hunt when I spent half a day stalking a horse that I thought was an elk!

In essence, this book is also instructional. It's often much easier to learn from the school of hard knocks. You can become a better hunter by reading and studying the experiences of others, whether the correct decisions were made or not.

I hope you're entertained by these recollections, and if you improve your hunting skills by learning from my tales, that's an extra bonus.

May all your hunts have happy endings, and remember, you don't have to kill an animal to have a great hunt. Be thankful that we're privileged in America to enjoy the sport of hunting. Not many folks around the world can do so.

Jim Zumbo · Cody, Wyoming

IT STARTED HERE

Wow...Do elk have saddles?!

There's a first time for everything. I can remember the first time I dove into a swimming pool, the first trout I ever caught, and the first girl I ever kissed.

And of course, I remember my first elk hunt. It wasn't exactly a memorable outing from the standpoint of success, but it was, nonetheless, a learning experience. And, as they say, experience is indeed the mother of learning. We become successful in life by learning from our mistakes.

This particular hunt was fraught with lots of mistakes. It took place in the '60's near Oak Creek, Colorado. As I recall, nonresident licenses were around $50 or so, and I was hunting with a couple relatives, neither of whom had any knowledge of the hunting units.

One of my relatives had friends in Oak Creek, and they were going to take us to their favorite spot. I was excited, because

Colorado was the hot spot for elk, and we were going to a super place loaded with big bulls. I couldn't wait.

Opening morning was most interesting. We were driven to the top of a mountain on a rocky, deeply rutted, pathway that someone called a road. I believe maybe a bulldozer had made one or two swipes over it, but we somehow got to the ridge, though we weren't sitting in the same positions in the Jeep when we arrived. When we left the bottom I was in the front; when we got to the top I was in the back, which was interesting in itself because there were about eight of us jammed in that little Jeep. It reminded me of the skit in the circus where a dozen or so clowns climb out of a Volkswagen.

When we arrived at the ridge, the strategy unfolded. I was told to jump out and hunt, and meet the Jeep driver after dark at a location that someone described by drawing a map in the sand next to the Jeep and illuminating it with a weak flashlight. I was to walk several ridges, work my way through several timbered slopes, and find "X", which was my rendezvous point.

I headed out in the dark, and had no idea what to do or where to start. If this was what elk hunting was all about, then I was about to be initiated.

The country was lovely, with lots of quaking aspen mixed with Douglas fir, alpine fir, and Engellmann spruce. I slipped through the trees slowly, looking for an elk, but I wasn't sure where to look, so I stillhunted along, carefully looking over every shadow and patch of brush, and stopping for several seconds to listen.

The buck showed up around 10 a.m. Apparently he'd been spooked by other hunters, because he was stepping out right smartly, running straight toward me. I was leaning against a big spruce tree, eating an apple.

That buck made me regret my decision not to buy a nonresident deer tag. The season opened along with elk, but I was a struggling young forest ranger, too broke to come up with the extra money for the deer permit.

I watched in frustration as the deer spotted me and stopped momentarily to stare. He was astounded at my presence, and it took him about two seconds to identify me and crash headlong into heavy timber.

To this day, that buck was one of the biggest I've ever seen in almost three decades of hunting muleys. I'll never forget the giant, massive rack as the deer disappeared into the forest.

Later, I got into a forest of spruce trees that had been heavily used by elk. Fresh droppings and tracks were everywhere. I eased around, absolutely sure that I'd see my six-point bull behind the next tree, but he never materialized. Nothing showed at all, despite the fact that I'd hiked all over the area for the next two hours.

With darkness coming on, I headed for the spot that I was supposed to meet the Jeep. On the way, I heard something crash through the timber in front of me. I couldn't see what was making the noise, but it sounded formidable.

The sounds finally petered out, and as I walked on, I discovered fresh elk tracks in the forest floor. I'd apparently blundered into a small herd, but they quickly became history.

The next day we tried another area, and my companion and I became involved in a hunt that I swore I'd never make public, unless, of course, I ever wrote a book on elk hunting that poked humor at my experiences. This is that book, so I'll reveal the story.

My companion spotted an elk across a wide canyon. The animal was standing in a patch of oak brush, and all we could see was part of its body.

We began a slow, careful stalk that took about four hours. Our tags were for bulls only; perhaps the critter we were sneaking up on was a bull, and maybe there were more of them out of sight.

As we narrowed the distance, I kept looking at the elk. It never moved from the pocket of brush, and I couldn't be sure if it was standing or bedded. I assumed it was bedded, because it had been in that spot for a long time.

At one point, I got a look at it from another perspective. I thought I saw something move, and kept looking.

The movement appeared again, and suddenly I made it out. The elk's long tail was swishing about now and then.

Elk, unfortunately, do not have long tails. Neither do deer, bears, or any other large critters in Colorado.

A horse..... Indeed, we had been stalking a buckskin horse that was tied to the brush. The horse was colored exactly like an elk.

My pal and I made a secret pact there and then to never tell a soul that we'd spent almost half a day stalking a horse. I have now broken that pact, with his approval, incidentally, only because it's good to laugh at ourselves now and then.

A couple days later, I was wandering along during a blustery, chilly day, when a snowflake hit my face. Another followed, and soon I was hunting in a dandy blizzard. The snow stopped an hour later, with a few inches piled on the ground.

At one point I saw the legs of two elk in brush ahead of me. The legs were blurred, because they were moving along at a dead run. I couldn't see the head of either animal, and watched as they disappeared in the trees.

I figured one of those elk would be meat on the table, if either wore horns. With perfect tracking snow, all I had to do was follow the smoking trail and shoot my bull.

I picked up the tracks in seconds and slowly followed. They headed through the forest in a straight line, and I noted the elk weren't detouring much around obstacles. They merely ran through or over them.

About 15 minutes later, the tracks took me to the edge of the forest where the timber broke away into a wide sagebrush valley. The elk had run out of the trees, and straight through the valley.

Since I'd never been in the area before, I didn't know the open valley existed. Had I been aware of it, I could have easily ran to the edge of the trees and had a shot at the escaping elk. Instead, I had been poking along at a snail's pace, following the tracks that I figured sooner or later would have an elk standing in them.

I was mad at myself, but not nearly so upset when my companion told me he'd been sitting in the Jeep when two big bulls charged out of the timber and practically jumped over the vehicle when the animals crossed the road. Apparently I'd seen the pair after they almost piled into the Jeep, about 400 yards into the timber.

Live and learn, as they say. I still pull some dumb stunts when I hunt elk, but I've never again stalked a horse. I said to heck with horse hunting forever more.

ELK HEAVEN AIN'T IN HELL'S CANYON

I should know better when someone invites me to hunt with borrowed or rented horses. Murphy's Law almost always prevails, and in this case it not only prevailed — it was very well done. Murphy got us good.

My good buddy Ed Iman had been trying to get me to hunt with him in Oregon's Hell's Canyon for years, but my good sense always kept me out of trouble. One evening, however, when Ed and I were relaxing after a day's fishing on the Columbia River, he caught me in a weak moment.

Oregon was one of the two states I hadn't hunted elk in, so I agreed to apply for a Hell's Canyon tag. I reasoned that it would be good for me to go, because I like to hunt different elk country every year. I'd heard lots about the famed canyon formed by the Snake River, so the deal was made. I'd apply for a tag.

Ed is a full-time fishing guide on the Columbia, and we've made a number of trips together. He's lucky for me, too, which was another reason I decided to go elk hunting with him.

One day, when we were fishing for walleyes, which are Ed's specialty, I told him I'd kiss his butt in Macy's front window during the noon hour if I caught a 10-pound walleye from his boat.

Two hours after my wager, which, of course, was made in jest, I landed a 12 1/2 pound walleye. I quickly retracted my offer, explaining that the statement was all in good fun. Ed was not amused by my reneging on the deal, and offered to pay the expenses to Macy's. So far I've successfully found a series of excuses to avoid the ill-conceived date. Even so, the last time I was in New York, I cautiously made sure I wasn't followed and carefully avoided the Macy's area.

Nonetheless, if I could catch the biggest walleye of my life with Ed, maybe I could kill a good bull with him...

We applied for tags, but weren't drawn for the first hunt. Those tags are always oversubscribed, so we accepted tags for the second hunt, which is never oversubscribed. Everyone who applies for the second hunt gets a tag, which should have been fair warning in itself. But I was committed, and there was no backing out. We'd hunt the second season which started in November.

Unfortunately, Ed and I were doing hunting and fishing seminars for the International Sportsmen's Exposition in Portland which overlapped the opener of our hunt. We'd have to miss the first few days, but Ed wasn't worried. After all, he'd hunted the area several times and knew where the elk were. Guaranteed, he told me.

Ed's pal, Richard, would accompany us. Richard had a couple horses of his own, and he'd borrow one from a neighbor. We'd rent two others, and head for the hills with five head.

It took us all day to drive from the Portland area to Hell's Canyon. Each of us drove a vehicle, with Ed in the lead. Richard had two horses in his truck and towed a horse trailer containing the other three.

It was slow going for our little caravan, and eventually Ed got us a little lost in the bottom of the canyon where we'd park the rigs, if we ever found the spot to park them. We were just slightly confused, however, and Ed had things unraveled in no time, just under what seemed like three hours. Soon we were at the trailhead where we watered the horses and turned them loose.

"Don't worry, they can't go far," Ed said.

Ed Iman looking over his damaged rifle, wondering why Murphy's Law struck so many times.

The horse we thought we lost wasn't lost at all. He just wandered off in the dark, but stayed inside the fenced area, which was only an acre or two. Ed found him with a flashlight, hiding along the willows near the creek. Apparently the horse knew what was coming and wanted nothing to do with us.

When the horses were tended, we ate an impromptu dinner and got around to discussing sleeping quarters. We intended to head up the trail at first light, and would overnight at the trucks.

Ed claimed he had the problem solved with a dandy tent he'd purchased for $20 in a recent garage sale. When he started rummaging for it in his van and muttered something about never having set it up before, I took the clue and quickly retrieved my trusty tent from my truck.

Ed was still looking for his tent when I calmly announced that mine was up and ready for sleeping bags. Ed muttered some more, but I couldn't make out what he said since his head was buried under 14 boxes of stuff stashed in his van. He heard me though, and reluctantly quit looking for his bargain tent. Richard and I secretly breathed a sigh of relief.

We were up early the next morning, and were on the trail long before the sun appeared over the high bluffs above us. Our destination was about 17 miles into the innards of the canyon. Ed claimed he knew of the perfect camp spot. Richard had hunted the general area before, but not where we were headed.

All seemed to be going well, until we left the lower elevations and started up the trail which wound around some fairly impressive cliffs. I've seen a good part of the Rockies, and this trail was no slouch when it came to nastiness.

At one point we were climbing up a steep slope when a rope on Ed's packhorse gave way. A sleeping bag tumbled out and fell under the horse, who suddenly panicked at the thing bouncing around underneath it. Ed's horse panicked too, and Ed jumped off. Unfortunately, Ed's rifle came off the horse too, falling out of the scabbard and ultimately under the hooves of the wild-eyed bucking horses.

When everything was finally under control, I quietly announced to Ed that his rifle had been smartly stomped upon. He hadn't seen it happen, and cussed a blue stream when he noted the scope had been badly knocked out of whack.

It was too late to head back. We continued to head to the camp area, and somewhere along the route, Ed mentioned that he'd forgotten to pack the grain for the horses. That being the case, he'd head back to the trucks in the morning to bring back the grain and get a spare rifle that was in his van. Somehow it seemed that the forgotten grain further justified his trip back to the trucks, but sometimes I never quite figure out Ed's logic.

Camp was not where Ed thought it was. We looked more, and finally found it, but the nearby water trough, that Ed said was ALWAYS full, had a mere two cups of water in it. Evidently the spring that fed it had dried up.

It was back on the trail to another campsite, this one another five miles away. Ed knew another hunter who always camped there; we'd just make camp next to his.

Darkness was just two hours away when we dropped into the timbered canyon where we'd camp. On the way down, we saw a couple cow elk that looked at us curiously. Seeing those elk inspired me — maybe we'd even see a bull after all. I'd been having my doubts.

We had the horses unpacked, watered, and staked in no time. It was still light out when we sat in front of the tent around a campfire and ate one of Ed's meals, which, incidentally, are actually very good. A couple of nice libations with our neighbors camped next to us induced sleep. It had been a long ride, and dreams came easy.

Long before daybreak, we had coffee and a light breakfast. Richard and I split up and headed for the ridgetops, while Ed saddled horses and rode out to the trucks. He'd be back the next day, after riding more than 35 miles on horseback, a task he generously made without comment, at least none I'd care to repeat in print.

The country was unique, unlike anything I'd ever hunted before. The slopes were extremely steep, and covered with cheatgrass. Visibility was unbelievably long.

Elk lived in the draws and canyons that held Douglas fir and brush. Because most of the timbered spots were high, we had to climb those torturous slopes to get to the trees.

I estimated that perhaps less than 15 percent of the area held elk cover. The rest of it was cheatgrass that would barely hide grasshoppers.

It took me the better part of two hours to climb from camp to a basin nestled between two mountains. The area was heavily forested, and looked perfect for elk.

Sitting on a slope where I could see into some of the small openings, I soon spotted elk, but they were all cows. I watched them for a long time, hoping that a bull might show up, but no luck.

I stillhunted the basin until noon, then headed for the ridgetop. I walked along it for two miles, and saw a few more cows. Every now and then I'd see hunters riding horseback on the numerous trails below.

A bunch of ravens alerted me to the remains of an elk taken by hunters on the first hunt. Only the skeleton was evident; apparently the hunters had boned the elk and hauled the meat out.   According to Ed's pals who were camped near us, hunters took 19 bulls the first season in the general area we'd hunted. That wasn't very good news for us, because elk cover was so limited that it could be thoroughly hunted over a short period. Few bulls escaped the first hunting period.

I also learned that big bulls were rare in the canyon. They simply didn't live enough years because harvesting was too consistent. Bulls had to have three points to the side to be legal — most of them taken by hunters were small four and five pointers.

Later in the afternoon, magpies pointed out three more elk remains, and I began to wonder if any legal bulls were left. I'd never seen such open country with so little cover, and it was evident that earlier hunters knew how to work the country effectively.

About two hours before dark I saw a cow bedded in the timber across the canyon. I watched her for a long time through binoculars, and she finally got up and moved along a contour up the canyon. With her were two more cows and a small bull.

As they walked, I kept up with them on my side. The canyon narrowed ahead, and I'd have an easy shot if the elk kept walking and the bull was legal.

The herd of animals disappeared in thick timber and I lost sight of them. Fifteen minutes later, while I walked along, I spotted them on my side of the canyon. In fact, they were just 60 yards below me in a grassy opening.

A cow winded me and barked. The herd ran off, but I quickly blew my cow call. Instantly the animals stopped and looked me over, giving me a chance to inspect the bull.

He wasn't terribly exciting. The elk had a fork and a very small tine about two inches long on one antler which made him legal. I debated a long time, but elected not to shoot. The bull was a yearling and would be outstanding meat on the table. I rationalized that this was the first day, and I might see something better.

The elk finally decided to leave, and I blew the cow call again when they disappeared. Later, when I walked farther down the ridge, I saw them feeding in about the place where they were when I'd last blown the call. Evidently it calmed them down and they resumed feeding.

I got to camp after dark, and started a fire. Richard walked in a few minutes later and we ate dinner, sharing the day's hunt and wondering how Ed would fare.

I was high on a ridge the next morning when a big bunch of elk ran by me, apparently pushed by another hunter. There was a spike bull in the group; the rest were cows and calves.

Ed came into view about midmorning, leading a packhorse down a series of switchbacks about two miles from where I sat. I watched him for a while, passing time until late afternoon when elk would start feeding.

The afternoon hunt was uneventful, and so was the rest of the week. Except for the small bull I'd seen on the first day, no one saw a legal animal. It had been a good hunt, however, with plenty of laughs and camaraderie.

One of the challenges was yet to come. It happened when we were heading out of camp. A packsaddle on one of the horses hadn't been snugged down correctly. Whenever the horse walked, the saddle dug into its hide, and the animal ran forward a few steps, constantly trying to overtake the lead horse.

Ed had the job of leading the horse, and when he started ahead on his saddle horse, the hurting pack animal lurched out in front.

I must admit the scene was funny. Ed was trying to stay ahead of the horse he was leading, but he was having a tough time, despite his cussing. None of us realized the problem; we thought the animal was just feeling a little feisty after not being used all week.

Finally Ed got the horse behind him where it belonged, and we headed up the trail. Unfortunately, we'd progressed only 100 yards when the packhorse suddenly lunged forward on the narrow trail.

The other horses pranced nervously, and the second packhorse, which had been behaving nicely, jumped about just enough to loosen its pack.

A wreck was in the making, when the now-startled second packhorse succeeded in bucking to the point where the pack completely slipped and rolled under its belly.

The animal was not fond of the situation. His eyes were as big as saucers, and the panicky animal dashed about wildly on the trail, kicking and stomping about.

Finally the horse lost its footing and slammed to the ground below the trail. Quickly Ed and I rushed over, using calm words to reassure the frightened horse. We worked quickly to loosen the pack, and soon had the horse completely unhitched.

The animal seemed to be okay, though he was a bit shaky. The first

horse, however, with the maladjusted packsaddle, was as nervous as a cat in a room full of rocking chairs. He was on the verge of causing another wreck, so I told Ed and Richard I'd lead the fool animal to the top of the mountain while they repacked the other horse.

Rather than ride my saddlehorse and try to lead the balky packhorse up the narrow trail, I elected to hike up afoot, and let Ed or Richard lead my horse when they got everything squared away

I started walking up the trail, and the horse was unhappy with our hike. I still had no idea the packsaddle was chafing his side, because the area that was being irritated was under the saddle. I assumed that the horse was a knothead, and making a jerk out of himself as many horses will do.

A couple times the horse almost pushed me off the trail, and he kept me moving at a smart step. The animal wouldn't slow down, and I didn't want to try to slow him down on the trail. As it was, I occasionally whacked him on the snout with the end of the halter rope, but that seemed to inspire him to walk quicker.

Finally the mountaintop came into view, and I was mighty relieved to reach the top of the ridge after the forced march. I was sweating profusely, and all my thoughts had been directed toward sending the idiot horse off to the glue factory.

While waiting for Ed and Richard, I looked the horse over, and discovered the sore under his packsaddle. A small area had been rubbed raw, and I understood why he'd been behaving badly.

A readjustment of the packsaddle corrected the problem, and we made it back to the trucks just before dark with no other incidents. We made camp again at the trucks, and when I asked Ed to look for his garage sale tent so we could try to set it up, he gave me a big grin.

"With all the bad luck we've had, Zumbo, I ain't about to ask for any more," he answered.

"We could've had worse luck and killed an elk," I said.

"How's that?" Ed asked.

"Can you imagine packing a bull out of there on these horses, and having more wrecks on the trail? We'd be in there a week just packing out meat," I said.

"That's the best justification I ever heard for not getting an elk," Ed responded. "You writers have all the right excuses."

At that Richard spoke up and made a profound statement.

"Why don't you guys stick to walleyes," he said. "That's more your style."

"Speaking of walleyes," Ed said, "there's a trip we need to make to Macy's, you know."

Some people really know how to hurt a guy. I pretended not to hear Iman, and went about my chore of putting up the tent.

PS. I love to poke fun at Ed Iman, but he's actually a fine outdoorsman. Our hunt just had a bunch of little things go wrong. I would hate, however, for him to know I think he's good in the outdoors. Maybe he won't read this book. Don't tell him about it if you fish with him.

I COULD HAVE BEEN A HERO

Diamond Mountain really isn't a mountain at all, but a series of ridges that grow from a high plateau. Most of the ridges are small mountains themselves, separated by draws and valleys that are fertile and lush with grass. The mountains are blanketed with quaking aspens, Douglas firs and ponderosa pines, and the poor soils in the lowlands support pinyons and junipers.

The mountain lies northeast of Vernal, which is in extreme

northeast Utah, not far from the juncture of Wyoming, Utah and Colorado. It is a picturesque region, with varying landscapes ranging from vertical colorful cliffs to deep gorges. In the lower elevations, greasewood deserts abound, some of them with pink, rose and purple mounds called gypsy's petticoats. Higher up, the land takes on heavy forests, rising finally to the High Uintas, a wilderness mountain range whose tallest mountains show white snow all year.

Diamond Mountain received its name decades ago when, as the story goes, some shysters planted phoney diamonds in order to sell the land at a high price.

Early homesteaders typically claimed the valleys on Diamond Mountain, ignoring the steep slopes and ridgetops. Today, many of the ridges are federal lands, managed by the Bureau of Land Management, which is an agency of the Department of Interior.

Because of ownership patterns, some of the best elk hunting on Diamond Mountain is unavailable to the public, even though most of the elk live on public land. The private property in the bottoms is posted, effectively blocking hunter access to the higher federal lands. This problem isn't unique to Diamond Mountain, incidentally, but is typical throughout the west.

Much of Diamond Mountain is open, with vast expanses of sagebrush. Roads are everywhere; it's almost impossible to get more than a mile away from a road.

Accessible public lands on the mountain are hammered by throngs of hunters, many of them from Vernal, but a good share from out of the area as well. Since Diamond Mountain is an easy half-hour drive from Vernal, it receives plenty of consistent pressure. Big bulls are uncommon; most taken are spikes and raghorns.

Hunters who are continually successful are related to or are friends of landowners. Most elk come from the private areas, or public lands blocked by deeded parcels.

I lived in Vernal for a number of years, and was never part of the "in" groups who had private land privileges. My buddies and I hunted BLM land, and more often than not were unsuccessful. We had to put up with crowds of hunters, and elk hunting became a frustrating experience — a race to get to the elk first.

It didn't take me long to figure out that I'd need to hunt other areas and states, so I turned to nearby Wyoming and Colorado for most of my elk hunting. Unfortunately, it was tough to draw a Wyoming nonresident tag, and Colorado was just as crowded as Utah on much of its public land. Now and then I hunted Diamond when I had a day or two to hunt.

It was about 1976 when my 12-year-old son Danny suggested we hunt on Diamond Mountain the last day of the season. I was busy with some projects around the house, and knew that the few bulls left on the mountain were dug in so well that we'd never root one out.

Danny was persistent, so I postponed my chores and we headed out long before daybreak. He was too young to hunt, but he loved tagging along after me, and I loved to hunt elk, so it didn't take much convincing for me to go.

As I drove to the mountain in the dark, I had no idea where to go. Every possible spot had been hunted thoroughly. While driving up, I could see the taillights of a dozen vehicles in front of me, and the headlights of a dozen behind me. I knew that by 8 a.m. the mountain would be crawling with hundreds of hunters.

I parked the truck near a place where a buddy had killed a six-point bull many years before. He had hiked around a bend, spotted the bull sleeping in its bed, and killed it where it lay. The story had been repeated dozens of times to the point where my friend was a local hero for taking a six-point bull on Diamond Mountain.

Though Danny and I walked along a ridge, through some timber, and poked around in forested pockets, we couldn't find any fresh sign. I'd expected as much, and was frankly looking forward to the end of the day. I knew the hunt would be futile.

We were driving down the road, looking for another place to hunt, when an oncoming vehicle slowed on the dirt road. I recognized the driver, a good friend of mine, and he told me he'd found a frozen waterhole that had been broken open by elk during the night. He had to get back to town to take some livestock to the auction, and couldn't hunt any longer.

I knew where the waterhole was and headed for it. Maybe by some stroke of luck a spike bull might be nearby.

It was dry and dusty, and the elk were needing water frequently. Sign at the waterhole revealed fresh tracks, though they were hard to discern on the frozen ground. Indeed the elk had stomped through the thin ice to get a drink.

With that evidence available, Danny and I climbed up into some rocky terrain to a small shelf that held juniper trees. As we climbed, hunters drove by aimlessly, no doubt wondering where to hunt on the last day. The waterhole was just 75 yards from the main road that the hunters were using, and the juniper shelf was barely 200 yards from the waterhole.

We had just reached the shelf when a sudden commotion in the junipers brought me to full attention. A cow and calf elk dashed through the cover, stopping in full view about 100 yards away. I watched the pair as they moved slowly back into the brush. I had only a bull tag.

"Mom has a cow tag," Danny said. "Why didn't you shoot the elk?"

I sat Danny down on a rock and explained laws and ethics. It wasn't uncommon for some hunters to shoot animals for other people, and some of Danny's friends had parents who did just that. He didn't realize it was both wrong and illegal, so I tried my best to make him understand the ethics of hunting.

After the little lecture, we continued on our way. I was still amazed that we'd seen the cow and calf. To see any elk at all on Diamond Mountain on the last day of the season was a major accomplishment, one that you told all your pals about.

We were easing through the junipers, and I wasn't paying attention to much of anything. I'd assumed the cow and calf made up the entire elk population on the shelf. The only track I made out clearly at the waterhole was a cow track, so there was no reason to expect any better. No doubt every bull within two miles of our location had been killed off by now.

What happened next was an experience whose memory returns to haunt me so regularly that I still remember every vivid detail. I saw an elk lying under a juniper tree, and our meeting was so sudden that the animal and I stared at each other in shock.

The elk's coat was light-colored, usually indicating a bull, but the sun was streaming through a slot in the foliage, hitting the elk's flank.

At this point in my story, you have probably figured out what I'm going to say, but let me continue.

Because of my lack of enthusiasm of hunting that day, I'd forgotten my binoculars. An important safety rule says never to point a firearm at something you don't intend to shoot, so I shouldered my rifle and aimed the scope above the elk's head. I was obeying the safety code by looking at air between the animal's ears, and was, of course, hoping to see antlers through the scope.

The elk stared at me with intensity that I'd never before seen in an animal. I'd caught it flatfooted, and it knew the danger of the situation. An air of electricity seemed to pass between the elk and I. The hair on the back of my neck stood straight out, and goosebumps rippled my arms and legs.

I stood there, riveted to the ground, alternately raising and lowering the scope, trying with all my might to see antlers. The elk's head was in the lower juniper branches, and at times I was positive I could see brow tines. The next moment I couldn't be sure.

If the elk would move it's head just a half-inch, that movement would betray antlers above, but the animal was as still as a statue.

The standoff ended when the elk suddenly sprang from its bed and leaped over the edge of the shelf, down toward a dense thicket. I quickly snapped my rifle up, but the elk had made the move in less than a second. When he jumped, he never hit the ground until he was down out of sight.

I made a mad dash for the shelf's edge, and caught my toe between two rocks. I went down to the ground hard, feeling extreme pain in my ankle, but pain and hurt were second priority.

I had seen great antlers flash when the elk exploded from the tree. Yes, it was a grand animal, perhaps the biggest bull alive on Diamond Mountain.

After regaining my footing, I rushed headlong for the edge, but the bull was gone. I heard him crashing through the junipers, but I never caught a glimpse of the animal.

I sat on a rock, and suddenly felt the pain in my ankle, but it didn't hurt as much as the emptiness in my heart. That big bull was a gift, an offering, and I'd blown it.

I thought about every detail of the confrontation, and rolled the scenario over and over in my mind. Like a Monday morning quarterback, I analyzed every one of my actions. I needed to blame something, but there were no culprits with the exception of not having binoculars.

Those doggoned binoculars! How could I have been so careless to forget them. I probably would have seen details that my four-power scope couldn't. Perhaps I could have clearly seen the antler configuration.

Maybe. And maybe not. As I sat on the rock, with an obvious sprained ankle, I went through it and through it. Over and over.

Danny had witnessed the entire episode. He'd been standing at my side when the bull and I had our staring match. Danny hadn't said a word throughout the confrontation, and I suddenly realized that he was gone.

I sat there a few moments longer, and started to see some humor in the situation. I hobbled over to the bull's bed, and from where he lay on the edge of the shelf, he could watch every vehicle pass by within 250 yards away. One of the biggest bulls on Diamond Mountain was lying in an arid patch of junipers and cactus, chewing his cud within easy rifle shot of a small army of hunters.

Then I hobbled over to where I had been standing and paced the distance between me and the bull.

Sixty-two feet. Sixty-two feet of space separated me from success that would have shocked the town. Instant fame. My name would have been a household word among Vernal's elk hunters.

I was still smiling when Danny yelled.

"Dad," he shouted, "come over here. Look what I found."

I walked over, favoring my ankle carefully, and saw him looking at the remains of a very nice five-point bull. The massive bleached rack lay in a pile of bones. From all indications, the animal had been dead for at least a year, perhaps wounded by a hunter, perhaps killed by a cougar, or maybe he'd died of starvation.

Nonetheless, I found it interesting that this bull, who was exceptional on Diamond Mountain, chose this very place to die, not 80 yards from where the other bull had been bedded.

The existence of both bulls indicated that there was something about the place that they liked. Undoubtedly it was the disturbance factor. Hunters didn't bother them in the unlikely spot, and the animals felt secure there. A closeby water source and plenty of feed beneath the ledge provided their daily requirements.

Danny asked if he could have the antlers as a souvenir of the hunt. I sent him back to the truck for a saw, and sawed them off the skull.

After packing the antlers the short distance to the truck, I drove slowly down the dusty road, looking back at the shelf which once held, as far as I knew, the king bull of Diamond Mountain.

I muttered to myself as I drove. "Sixty-two feet. No binoculars. Sixty-two....."

"What did you say, Dad?"

"Nothin' much, son. To heck with it."

Jim Zumbo on a favorite horse.

FOREST OF TERROR

Keep Cussin' and I'll find you!

Hunting elk on horseback is often a most fascinating experience. If done correctly, the rider heads out of camp in the dark, long before daylight. At day's end, the hunter rides back to camp, again in the dark.

The word "dark" conjures a poorly lit scene. When I say dark, I mean pitch-black dark, like being in an unlighted closet or room with no windows and the door closed. You put your hand in front of your face but you see nothing. You move your hand closer to your face, and you still see nothing, only total, absolute, blackness.

That's precisely the kind of dark I'm talking about when you ride back to camp through elk country on a horse when the sun is long gone from the western horizon and overcast skies block the moon and starlight. The horse moves about, and you sit on its back, having no idea in the world where you are.

You seem to be in space, riding in a galaxy of billions of black atoms. An aura of nothingness surrounds you as you sit in the rocking, creaking saddle.

During this period of impossible darkness, you hope like heck for two things: that your horse has the best night vision of all the jillions of other horses in the world, and that an invisible branch doesn't reach out like dracula's hand and sweep you off the saddle.

I've been in lots of dark-dark situations, but the most vivid occurred while riding one particular stretch of trail in Idaho's Selway with outfitter Ken Smith. This pathway, which is located in what is fondly known to Ken and I as the Forest of Terror, winds about in the bottom of a draw underneath huge cedar trees. The cedars have canopies so thick they block out starlight, moonlight, and even a lot of the sunlight during the day.

My first hunt with Ken was late in the year. The elk season in his part of the Selway ran from mid-September to Thanksgiving weekend. I opted for the latter, hoping for snow to help our hunt.

Ken's unit is about as remote as you can find in the Selway. To get to it, you must fly in to a grass strip located in the midst of the wilderness.

Interestingly enough, a wilderness area isn't supposed to be accessible to motorized vehicles and craft, but the strip was in place long before the area became a wilderness, so the aircraft restriction was exempted. Besides, a ranger station is next to the strip, requiring an airplane ride to get to and from it.

I flew out of Orofino, Idaho, with a pilot that Ken was high on. I was glad Ken liked him, because other people told me about the wilderness strip. It was no piece of cake, I was advised, requiring a dive into a canyon followed by a U-turn over a timbered ridge in the bottom, and then a series of turns and small dives to line the plane up with the strip.

The pilot did a great job, and I was impressed with the tricky maneuver. He had made the trip in the strip hundreds of times, and obviously was not a bold pilot. As the old saying goes, there are old pilots, and there are bold pilots, but there are no old, bold pilots.

I've been in plenty of bush planes in the north country; this ride was one of the kind you talk about later on, especially since the cruise over the forest as we flew toward the strip was iffy in itself. Big nasty clouds in the distance were hanging over mountaintops causing unflyable conditions, but our route was clear enough for safe flying.

Ken's base camp is located at the strip. He was waiting for me when the plane landed, and we wasted no time packing gear and heading for the Forest of Terror, which, of course, I had no idea about, and if I did, I might have said to heck with elk hunting right there and then.

A four-hour horseback ride put us into hunting camp. In short order I was shown to my tent, introduced to other hunters and guides, and settled in for the duration.

A meal by Elizabeth, Ken's cook (who later became his wife), was superb, and I fell asleep with a smile on my face, an elk tag in my pack, and lots of hope for the morning.

We were on the horses long before the sun was a glimmer in the east. I climbed aboard the frosty saddle, and we headed off across several ridges.

The Selway is beautiful in the winter, presenting a panorama that could easily be an artist's delight for splendid western wintry Christmas scenes. It was a winter wonderland every place you looked.

Our strategy was to ride to certain lookout points, tie up the horses well away from the vantage spot, and watch for elk in burned areas that were open enough for good visibility.

I don't remember seeing country that looked so good, but we never spotted animals that day. I was confident that, over the next few days, our time would come and we'd see elk.

Ken and I rode in another direction the next morning, and I was introduced to the Forest of Terror. The ride through it wasn't quite so bad, because the sun had already started up when we got to the forest and there was a bit of light in the trees.

Our plan for the day was to make a very long ride to a burned area that always held elk. We'd arrive by 10 or 11, and just sit and watch until dark. If an interesting bull showed, we'd make our move accordingly.

When we arrived, we tied our horses to trees and walked out to a good vantage spot. It was a beautiful day, with clear skies and crispy cold temperatures.

We had just eaten our lunches when we changed locations and spotted a bunch of elk directly below the ledge we were standing on. There were about a dozen or more, and they were hardly 150 yards away.

I spotted a small bull in the group, and looked at Ken.

"What do you think?" I whispered.

"It's your decision," he said with a grin. "It depends on how bad you want to go fishin'."

Ken also guides anglers for giant steelhead trout on the Clearwater River below Dworshak Dam. He'd told me that if I'd killed a bull early in the hunt we could leave camp early, fly out, and head for the river.

I looked at the elk, started to position my rifle for a shot, and changed my mind.

"We can always go fishin'", I said to Ken, "but right now we're elk huntin'. Let's keep on elk huntin' 'till we see a big mean old bull."

"I like your way of thinkin'", Ken answered. "Let that little guy grow up."

We sat there for several more hours, and about 3 o'clock Ken's prediction came true. Elk started drifting out of the timber and into the open burn to feed.

Within a half hour, there seemed to be elk everywhere. The open slopes across from us were full of animals, as they continued moving out of the brush and into the foraging areas.

I strained my eyes looking through glasses, and saw a few bulls, but none of them were really big. Some were branch-antlered, but the kind of big boy I was looking for wasn't in sight.

There was about a half hour of light left when I spotted a lone

This bull required us to make our way through the Forest of Terror but he was worth it.

animal in a narrow finger shaded by brush. He was partially hidden by trees, but the alpenglow rays from the sinking sun glinted off an antler.

This elk seemed really big, definitely worth a good look. I called Ken over, who was about 20 yards away, glassing another slope.

I pointed out the bull, and we both watched until the animal finally moved out into the open to where we could both see his antlers.

Wow!

That's about all I can say to describe our reaction. Simply wow! He might not have been a contender for the record books, but he was a dandy.

It was too late to move on him that day. He was fully three-quarters of a mile away; it would take several hours to get on him.

Ken and I watched until dark, then mounted our horses and headed back to camp. By the time we got to the Forest of Terror, it was good and dark, just right for things to reach out and touch you. We were about to enter the Inner Sanctum.

There are a few obstacles that make the F of T more interesting, or maybe the word terrifying would be a better term. One is The Log that lies across the trail. It's high enough that a tall horse can carefully walk over it, but some horses consider themselves great jumpers. They bunch their feet and make a sudden leap, clearing The Log with plenty of room to spare.

Ken's horse was tall. The beast simply walked carefully over The Log that was about two feet off the ground. My horse was tall, too, but unfortunately he was a leaper.

Now then, it is my opinion that every horse is a knothead to some degree. I say this, having owned a half dozen of the critters over the years. My horse was a bit of a knothead, but at least he had acceptable night vision. For that I was grateful.

Another obstacle is The Stream Crossing. As you sit there in absolute blackness, your horse suddenly plunges a couple feet down, and a mighty splash indicates he's jumped off the bank and into the stream, which he wades across, and then he makes another mighty jump up the bank on the other side.

Of course, you don't know The Stream Crossing is coming up. It's a very quiet stream, but you indeed become instantly aware of its presence when the saddle suddenly falls beneath you as your horse jumps off the bank.

The Low Branch is another fun treat in the F of T. This confounded branch is a small appendage from a fir tree that is not big enough to hurt your head, but merely knocks your hat off as you

'We head down to the Forest of Terror to pack out my bull.

come to it. I think Ken leaves The Low Branch there just to humor himself after an otherwise boring day in the elk woods. I believe The Log is another part of his masterplan to snicker and chuckle quietly as his hunter has confrontations with the various obstacles.

Another nifty aspect of the F of T is that Ken has a strict rule about using flashlights while riding. This is a major no-no, because a light will affect your horse's night vision. When The Low Branch swishes your hat off, Ken relaxes the rule, allowing you to use your light to dismount and look for your hat, which may be under, alongside of, or behind the horse.

You may not, however, use your light to determine the presence of The Log, The Branch, or The Stream Crossing. You simply guess as to when those items will show up and get you.

Ken always knows when The Log is encountered. My cussing tells him exactly where I am, and my good outfitter pal laughs himself silly as he rides up the trail. Luckily there are no low branches near The Log, because my horse leaps at least 12 feet into the air to clear The Log.

Getting back to the hunt, we successfully maneuvered through the F of T that evening. It would have been a little more tolerable if my horse hadn't been standing on my hat when The Low Branch knocked it off, but I managed to jostle, shove, and finally lift the horse's leg just enough to retrieve my newly redesigned Stetson. It was an old hat, anyway, and needed some more character and personality.

The next day, Ken and I headed back for the burn. By 2 in the afternoon, a bunch of elk had come out to feed, but we couldn't see the bull from the ridge where we were glassing from. Most of the elk we saw, including the big bull, were probably on another slope across a timbered valley.

The logical plan was to leave our horses on the ridge, cross the valley afoot, and get closer to where we'd last spotted the bull.

There was, however, a very important problem. Elk were everywhere, and we had to get through them in order to approach the place where the bull had been. Spooking the elk would have been a profound error, since they in turn could very well alert Mr. Big Boy that we were hoping to collect.

Ken and I had just started off the ridge when a cow barked within 100 yards of us. Great start!

She barked a dozen times and we saw her with her nose to the air, stepping cautiously about, as several other cows and calves followed. Another cow barked from another direction, and then yet another cow.

It was a cow-barking symphony. I never heard anything like it before. They reminded me of a bunch of dogs howling together in a chorus.

The cows finally broke and ran, but they luckily didn't head toward the slope where we figured the bull was. Ken and I proceeded across the valley, but first we agreed that the place we just left would be forever known as Cow-Barking Ridge.

It took a good hour to ease across the valley, and up a timbered slope to where we could look into the spot where we hoped the big bull might be. As we slipped up to the ridgetop, we saw dozens of elk feeding along the hillside.

Ken and I saw the bull at the same time, and the elk saw us too. They started running, and my first shot missed the big bull. Another bullet was on target, hitting the elk and breaking his back.

I'll never forget what happened next. He plunged to the ground, and fell down the slope. As his momentum picked up, he rolled faster and the slope got steeper. Finally, his body literally left the ground and he fell through the air, traveling 10 yards before hitting the ground again. He landed head-first in the bottom of the draw that was heavily choked with alders.

I was sure his antlers were smashed to bits as we headed over. For sure he was in a nasty spot.

It took us 20 minutes to get to where he lay, and as we were carefully making our way to him, an animal crashed out of the brush in front of us. A big whitetail buck exploded through the cover. I had no deer tag, and if I had, it would have been a most interesting double-header provided I hit the buck.

The bull was crumpled in a horrid tangle of alders. It was tough to see his antlers because his body was covering part of them, but I finally made out seven points on one side and six on the other. He

One of Ken's guides get ready for a ride in the Selway.

was enormous of body too, and was, and still is, one of the heaviest bulls I've ever killed. We figured he'd go 900 or better on the hoof.

He was also in the worst place I've ever seen an elk expire. Ken and I had a major chore awaiting us.

It took us almost two hours to cut away the trees so we could position the bull for field dressing. It was almost dark when we started the task, and we had to finish the job by flashlight.

The walk out was not a stroll through the park. We negotiated thick brush and climbed an extremely thick slope, using flashlights to guide our way. Finally we got to the horses, and mounted up for the ride back.

I noted it was a very dark night, almost pitch black in the open. The Forest of Terror awaited us.

Somehow we managed to survive the F of T. Ken even became a considerate person, telling me when we were about to approach each of the obstacles. Perhaps he was so pleased with my bull that he decided to temporarily give me a break from the evil objects of the F of T.

The next day we led two pack mules to the fallen bull. It took most of the day to get the mules to the elk, and it was again dark-dark when we arrived in camp. I was so tired I didn't eat dinner that Elizabeth kept for us. All that mattered was a sleeping bag and quickly getting into a horizontal position.

Ken, Elizabeth, and I took the meat out the following day, and arrived at base camp at midnight. At one point during our trip out, a packmule carrying the bull's heavy front shoulders decided to jump over a freshly-fallen tree in the trail on a steep sidehill.

Ken was most unhappy with the unexpected maneuver, primarily because the mule unbalanced its cargo. Ken and I struggled to unload the mule and repack him. It took an hour of tough work, and the mule was the subject of hundreds of words that Ken and I muttered, none of which can be printed.

On the flight out, I asked the pilot if the Forest of Terror was close to our flight path, and if so, to point it out to me.

When he asked why, I told him I was curious to know if there really was a sky over the top of it.

HUNTING UFO'S, TROPHY BLUE GROUSE, ILLEGAL BEARS, AND EVEN ELK

As Soon as yuh find a good huntin' spot, everyone finds out about it!

I know a place where elk are thick, but very few people hunt it, even though it's public land. The area is a lovely basin that resembles a horseshoe. The insides are moderately sloped, and covered with stands of aspen, Douglas fir and lodgepole pine.

On the outside of the basin, brutal mountainsides plunge deeply to the valley floor. Past fires created nightmare tangles that defy all but the most enthusiastic humans, one of them being me.

The open part of the horseshoe is almost flat, with a road leading up it into the basin. A locked gate precludes the public from entering the basin from the open part. A landowner has three 40-acre chunks of land in the bottom, entirely blocking access.

An enterprising hunter, however, can climb the steep walls on the outside of the basin and, once over the top, hunt to his or her heart's content. All one had to do was avoid the three 40's in the bottom, which was easy to do, because the 40's are open pastureland.

One of the few water sources in the basin is a pond on one of the 40's. The landowner and a few of his selected buddies killed elk every year by taking a stand in brush near the waterhole. Invariably, elk would head for water just before dark, and the successful hunter merely backed his pickup to the carcass and loaded the animal.

I started hunting the basin for a couple good reasons. First, it was plumb full of elk, but getting one meant cutting it into tiny pieces and backpacking it over the top. Getting a horse into the basin was a herculean chore because of the steep outside slopes, no trails, and a lack of water. The landowner would be mighty cantankerous if a hunter trespassed on his land to water a horse in the pond.

The second reason was because of a mean character in town who reminded me of a bully I knew in grade school. The mean guy was a friend of the landowner's, and he usually killed a bull every year off the waterhole. It would have been tolerable if he just told us about it, but he gloated over each kill, telling me and my pals how he parked the truck in the brush, walked 75 yards so he could see the waterhole, and have an elk dead in a half hour. Then he'd grin and tell us how he struggled terrible bad to get the giant bull in his truck.

I felt really sorry for the guy, considering all the hard work that went into his waterhole hunts. So sorry, in fact, that I set upon a scheme to complicate his tough hunts. I didn't want him to hurt his back loading all those elk in his truck.

The plan was to hike the miserable slopes into the basin and keep the elk stirred up so bad that they wouldn't go to the waterhole until after dark. While I was at it, I might even kill a bull myself just for the heck of it.

The back and highest part of the basin has a slick saddle that is a perfect crossing for elk. When the landowner and his friends start hunting the timber around the waterhole on opening morning, many of the elk head straight for the saddle where they'd cross and head down into the steep, terrible busted timber on the outside.

By sitting in the saddle, I'd be able to ambush an elk, which I occasionally did, but more often than not I didn't. Whether I did or didn't, I made sure I crisscrossed the basin real good just so the elk would know somebody was messing around. They wouldn't go to water if they figured the coast wasn't clear down around the three 40's.

I said to heck with elk hunting every time I climbed up into the basin. Each trip I swore I'd find a better route, but I never did. To make matters worse, a big, horrid rockslide blocked the way. Not only did I have to fight the jungles, I had to mince along across the rocks, some of them as big as my pickup truck.

The jungle was pretty interesting. Imagine yourself being an ant and trying to cross a bunch of pickup sticks lying in a heap. You'd never touch the ground, but would tightrope each stick. That's about what you had to do in the jungle.

I made the trip many times, usually by myself. It was my little private spot and I didn't want the word out. A few other hunters besides the landowner and his friends got into the basin, but those were rare visitors. Every now and then, however, I took a buddy in with me, but he was sworn to secrecy.

My standard procedure was to climb into the basin, leaving my truck parked at the bottom about noon. I'd take my time, resting frequently. I was carrying a 55-pound backpack, and wasn't in a hurry to wrench my back or develop a hernia.

I camped under a pair of Douglas fir trees about 400 yards downwind of the saddle. There was a natural bed of soft fir needles under the trees, and I pitched my mountain tent in precisely the same spot every year. Occasionally, when the weather was good, I didn't put up the tent at all, but slept under the stars. I didn't make a campfire because I didn't want the smoke to alarm the elk, so I normally climbed into the sleeping bag and watched the stars as soon as it got dark.

One night, as I lay on the peaceful mountaintop, I was looking up at the sky and saw a strange something that was much brighter than the other stars. Figuring it was an airplane, I kept watching, but it remained motionless. I stared at it for about 30 seconds and my brain started concocting some funny notions. I started thinking I saw green and red lights on the bright object, which someone once told me was characteristic of UFO's.

Now then, as you read this you might be chuckling to yourself and thinking I was hallucinating, but I can tell you that when I was lying there alone on that dark ridge with the closest humans about two miles away, I began to wonder about what I was looking at.

I reached over for Bertha, my .30/06 rifle that had been my constant companion for about 20 years, and laid it on my chest. If that funny light came any closer and little green people came toward me, they'd learn about 165-grain bullets real quick.

I didn't need to shoot any of them, however, because the light winked out when I wasn't looking. Maybe the thing was one of those Air Force balloons that the government traditionally uses as an excuse to explain funny things in the sky. Probably so, but I didn't sleep too well, until I heard a bull elk bugle down in the basin about midnight. Then I rolled over and went to sleep.

One day, when I was hunting near the bottom of the basin, I saw a brown-colored animal in the brush. It was coming up the same trail I was walking down on, so I quickly side-stepped the trail and moved about 10 yards away. I didn't know what the animal was, because I caught only a glimpse of it. The color looked about right for an elk, but I couldn't be sure.

Moments later the critter appeared on the trail. It was a light brown-colored bear, and I watched in amazement as it nonchalantly sauntered up the trail, never paying attention to my scent that must have been on the trail where I'd walked.

I smiled as the animal disappeared, because bear season had closed the day before. If I'd seen him one day earlier, he'd have been history and I'd have packed out a potential bear rug and good meat.

About a half hour after I'd seen the bear, a hunter appeared and seemed a bit irritated with my presence.

"How'd you get in here?" he asked. "The bottom is private land and is posted."

"I came in over the top," I answered. "I walked in on public land, every inch of the way."

I had recognized the hunter, and knew he was a friend of the man who owned the three 40's in the bottom.

The man turned to leave, and then stopped.

"Didn't you see that bear that came up through here a while ago?" he asked.

"Yep," I said. "It passed me by about 10 yards."

"Why didn't you shoot it?" the man asked.

"Season closed yesterday, my friend," I responded.

"That don't matter," he announced. "Bears kill my friend's sheep. We shoot bears whenever we see 'em. I'd have shot the one here, but it got away in the timber too quick."

"Good for the bear," I said. I gave the man a broad smile and headed back up the mountain. As I walked, I knew that the hunter no doubt figured I was the biggest jerk in the world, but I don't remember ever being so content with myself. It had been a very good morning.

I have a good pal who is an avid elk hunter, but he hasn't had much luck in the elk woods. Maybe he hunts too fast, or he hunts the wrong places. I decided to take him into the basin with me. Maybe he'd luck into a bull.

When we left my truck and started climbing, my buddy suggested we split up and meet at the top. He's a fitness freak, and in a lot better shape than me. I described to him where the two fir trees were, and told him to meet me there in about three hours.

As I already mentioned, the mountain we had to climb was blanketed with nasty cover generated by the fire. Some of the cover is just plumb nasty, and some of it is terrible nasty. I knew how to avoid the real bad stuff, but my buddy didn't. Since his pride wouldn't allow him to follow me up the mountain, I figured maybe I should fail to tell him exactly how to get around the worse of the thickets. What the heck — I have pride, too.

I beat him to the fir trees by 45 minutes. He showed up bleeding from several scratches, and his clothes were torn pretty good, too. He was surprised to see that I had made it up before him, but he didn't say a word. Sometimes silence is golden.

The next morning I posted him so he could see the saddle, and I made it plain that we should sit there until 9:30. If elk were going to show, they usually did so by 8:30, but I gave them an extra hour's margin.

I sat about 150 yards away from my pal, watching another part of the saddle. It was opening day, and I was confident that hunters in the bottom would push elk through the saddle and over the top. Elk usually headed for the bad thickets; they were almost impossible to hunt when they got in that stuff.

About 8:45 I heard a branch snap. I looked and saw my buddy wandering off through the timber. I shook my head, but I didn't want to disturb the woods by charging after him or shouting that he should stay put.

At 9:15 I heard another branch snap. Two bull elk ran toward me, a spike and a raghorn. Before I could get my gun up, they disappeared into the trees and that was it. The elk had been coming from the same direction they'd always come from, and if my pal had been where he was supposed to be, he'd have easily nailed one of the bulls.

Unfortunately, that incident occurred several years ago, before I knew the value of cow calling. Had I used a cow call, I'm 100 percent sure I could have stopped those running bulls long enough to get a shot.

I waited another hour, and eased into the trees, working the basin slopes. Around noon I heard a rifle shot, and I was almost sure it was my pal. Hurrying toward the direction of the shot, I found him plucking a neatly beheaded blue grouse.

I cussed my pal thoroughly for disturbing the elk woods that we had to ourselves, and for causing me untold excitement at the prospect of seeing him standing over a dead bull. Then we sat on a log and had a good laugh.

We split up and I heard him shoot about three hours later. Confident that he'd shot an elk, I ran toward him again, and this time found him chasing a blue grouse that he'd winged. I should have been mad, but the sight was so funny I laughed myself silly. He finally caught and dispatched the grouse. He explained that he simply couldn't resist shooting grouse for camp meat, because that's traditional. When I reminded him that we wouldn't be building any fires to cook the grouse at camp, he agreed to refrain from shooting any more birds in the basin. As it turned out, we were able to keep the birds cool until we got back down to the truck, so they weren't wasted. Neither of us got a shot at an elk for the duration of the hunt, but we had a good grouse barbecue in my back yard when we got home.

The moral to that hunt was to never investigate my pal's shots again. A few years later, when we were hunting mule deer, I heard him shoot but I refused to check him out. He'd killed a big old buck and worked all day to get it to camp by himself.

"How come you didn't come over when I shot?" he said when I strode into camp. "I about killed myself off dragging that buck to the road."

"Shucks, ol buddy," I said. "I didn't think you needed much help hauling a blue grouse back to camp. They only weigh but two pounds."

One year, me and my buddy and two other friends went into the basin from another approach. One of the guys had gotten permission from a rancher to cross his property and take horses up the outside of the basin. The route was about a mile from the two firs. The rancher also said we could water our horses on his property, which meant a long ride out of the basin and down into the valley on the outside. We figured it was worth it, and rode in on our horses about a week before elk season to find a place to camp.

We were riding through thick timber on a scouting mission before the season opened, when a bull bugled in front of us. We halted our horses and I whistled. The bull came unglued and charged straight toward us. We watched in amusement as he broke out of heavy cover and spotted us. The old boy skidded to a stop and almost fell over himself getting out of there.

No doubt the bull heard us coming and figured we were a herd of elk. The wind was in our favor and he just bounced right in for a look.

When elk season drew near, we rode in to the camp spot we'd located, and settled in for the night. My pal and I put up a small tent, just in case it stormed. Weather forecasters said it could rain in the evenings.

Our other two pals elected to sleep under the stars, and when we all turned in there was much discussion about me and my buddy being lightweights, afraid to sleep outside. A lot of talk went back and forth, and I finally dozed off around 11 p.m.

It was about 2 a.m. when the rain came, and it came fast and hard. Unfortunately, me and my pal were not taking any guests into our tent, and we laid there laughing hysterically while our two he-man companions attempted to erect their tent in the total blackness.

They were drenched when they got the job done, and their down sleeping bags were also drenched, clammy, and cold. It had been one of the most enjoyable nights I'd ever spent in the woods.

THEY PUT TROY ON THE MAP

"EXTRA" "EXTRA"!

There was a time when elk didn't have much going for them. Sure, there were hunters like you and me who cared, and plenty of photographers and plain wildlife viewers, too. For sure, western game departments managed elk so there'd be enough animals around, but nobody ever really did anything grand for elk on a large scale. There were no organizations that took the bull by the horns, so to speak, and worked hard for elk and their future on this planet.

Now there IS such an organization, and I'm glad to say it's flourishing beyond everyone's wildest dreams. As I write this, more than

70,000 people have joined its ranks in just six years, and it's conservatively estimated that the organization will be 500,000 strong before this decade runs out.

Were the founders of the ROCKY MOUNTAIN ELK FOUNDATION a bunch of esteemed college professors who were concerned about elk?

Nope.

Was the RMEF formed by a group of wealthy hunters as they sat in a 5-star restaurant drinking dry Bombay martinis with a twist or Absolut on the rocks?

No.

RMEF came to being because of four regular guys who lived in a little Montana town called Troy that almost nobody ever heard of. The foursome included a realtor, logger, cafe owner, and a preacher.

It was in the spring of 1984, when they were sitting around talking about nothing important, when the subject of elk came up.

The conversation went something like this:

"Somebody oughta do something for elk, you know, like Ducks Unlimited does for ducks."

"Good idea, but how do you go about it?"

"You start an organization and raise money."

"Sounds good, but who starts the organization to raise the money?"

"Maybe we can."

Silence.

Finally somebody pipes up. "You kidding? Here, in Troy, Montana– a town that has no traffic light and where we gotta drive 18 miles to Libby to go to the bank? Nobody'd take us serious."

More silence.

The discussion continues, and the four men go home to sleep on it. They agree to debate the idea again.

As their talks continue, they become more and more enthusiastic. Yes, they'd do their best to start an organization to go to work for elk.

They were immediately confronted with a problem.

Money.

To begin, three of them came up with $8,000 each, which would give them a tiny start. Little did they know that in just a few years their modest contribution would grow to an organization handling millions of dollars in its fund-raising efforts.

Bob Munson, his brother Bill, Charlie Decker and Dan Bull were the foursome that founded RMEF. Their initial months were fraught with unbelievable dilemmas and frustrations, but they persisted, despite the overwhelming odds against their success.

The first objective was to come up with a core of members. Easier said than done.

"We obtained 35,000 names of elk hunters from Colorado," Bob Munson recalled, "and we believed they were the names of successful hunters. We hired high school girls to send out mailings to 2,000 of the hunters. The girls placed little yellow sticky notes on each mailout with a personal congratulations to each hunter. Imagine our embarrassment when we learned that the hunters were NOT successful at getting an elk, but were merely successful at getting a LICENSE. By figuring the Colorado odds of getting an elk, some 1700 of the 2000 respondents were no doubt thinking we were crazy."

"We tried another mailing to 43,000 hunters," Munson continued. "We were optimistic, because we'd hired a consulting firm in Spokane who had studied the number of people responding to gravesite ads. The consultant said the typical response should be around 3 percent, but they believed we'd get 10 percent because our mailings were going to a targeted audience. As it turned out, we got 3/4 of one percent. We were so enthusiastic about the returns that we bought a $15 automatic letter opener. We didn't have to use it for two years."

Other mistakes were made. Today they're amusing to recall. When they happened six years ago, they were devastating.

The first membership decal, for example, turned black a week or two after it was placed on a window. Early membership cards were so flimsy the lamination separated almost immediately when they were put in a wallet. A large number of inexpensive "bronzestone" sculptures were so poorly made that they fell apart during shipping.

Early on, the founders knew they needed a magazine, but there wasn't anyone in Troy who knew much about the editing and publishing business.

"I know a guy who works for the Forest Service in Libby," said one of Bob Munson's friends. "He knows all about slides and stuff – maybe he can help out."

Bob looked up the government employee, Lance Schelvan, who was sort of known as the slide-show guru around those parts. He asked Lance if he'd like to work part time and produce their first magazine that they'd call BUGLE. Lance agreed, and worked out of his home with his wife, Lois.

"We got a quote from a printer in Spokane to print the first magazine," Bob said. "We accepted his bid, but the printer slipped a digit in his quote and we had to break the contract. Lucky for us, we found Hart Press in Minnesota. They printed the first BUGLE, and they've been with us to this day."

"We weren't terribly sophisticated," Lance said. "When Hart Press tried to print the first magazine, our boards were so full of scotch tape that the light reflected back to the camera. Because of little mistakes like that, we slowly learned how to turn out a quality magazine."

The first BUGLE was a challenge of immense proportions.

"We had 35,000 printed," Lance recalled. "We had no chance to look at the blue lines (final proof), and relied entirely on the printer."

"Funding for the first issue was tough," Bob Munson said. "Lucky for us, we had some supporters. John Marmaduke, an airline pilot, loaned us $25,000."

"When the shipment of magazines was delivered," Munson continued, "we drove to Missoula to pick them up. John went with us. At 9 o'clock on a Sunday morning, we pulled up to the 18-wheeler semi that carried our magazines. We had a pickup and towed a U-haul, and were absolutely flabbergasted when the truckdriver opened the doors and we saw the three enormous pallets loaded with BUGLES."

"What the hell do we DO with all those things?" someone said. It was a good question.

Marmaduke opened up a pallet and looked at one of the BUGLES. "Holy _____," he said. "This magazine will NEVER sell."

"We had no idea what to do with them", Munson admitted. "We had attracted just a few members, and we had a whole bunch of magazines to get rid of."

While driving back to Troy with knots in his stomach, Munson stopped at the Town Pump gas station in Thompson Falls. He talked the manager into accepting 20 copies on consignment. With that nifty transaction completed, only 34,980 more copies had to be disposed of.

"We sent free copies to 4,000 game license agents around the west," Munson said. "We invited them to order more copies, hoping to get a bunch of BUGLES sold, but only 1% of the agents responded. We sold about 400 copies. Obviously, there were a whole lot more to peddle."

"My brother Bill and I tried a telemarketing venture," Bob Munson stated. "For two weeks solid we called every game license agent we could, and got rid of 10,000 copies. They were on consignment though, and we had no idea as to how many would actually sell."

"Our big break came in Denver," Munson continued. "I called a wholesale distributor 24 times, but I could never make contact with him. His secretary either put me on hold, or told me he was busy or in a meeting. It got to be so frustrating. I nicknamed the secretary the 'iron maiden'. On the 25th call, I finally got through to the wholesaler. With a gruff, impatient voice, he told me he'd take 2,000 copies, then he promptly put me back on hold. I was delighted, and I'm glad to say that those first Colorado markets had a high success with BUGLE. We were on our way, but we really didn't know it at the time."

Bob and his wife, Vicki, were raising six children at the time. "During one trip," Vicki said, "while driving one of our sons to college in California, Bob stopped at every store he could and tried to sell copies of BUGLE. Our son was mortified, but Bob was undaunted."

Munson had hired a secretary to help the fledgling organization along. "He bought the first computer in Troy," Vicki said, "but the secretary didn't know how to use it. It sat in the little office, gathering dust. Finally I decided to take it home and figure it out. When I did, I pitched in to help and I've never quit."

When Bob and his pals formed the organization, they really didn't know exactly what to do for elk. They had an idea, but none of them were schooled in wildlife biology. One day, Bob had the opportunity to meet with Jack Ward Thomas, who is one of the top wildlife biologists for the U.S. Forest Service.

"I'm really happy you guys started this organization," Thomas said to Munson, "and I know why."

Never missing a beat, Munson jumped right into the conversation. "Why do you think we started it, Jack?" Munson asked.

Jack Ward Thomas responded, and Munson made mental notes. Now he knew what the mission of RMEF was.

And so it went. Little by little, Bob and Lance figured out how to play the game. Charlie Decker hung in with them, providing moral support and lots of laughs. Charlie, who is a logger, could easily pass off as Paul Bunyan. He is a burly man who you would be comfortable with in any saloon in Montana, yet he is a gentle person with a deep love of elk and the outdoors.

"A lot of credit should go to people who helped us financially," Munson said. "Wayne Haines, a banker from Libby and an avid elk hunter, believed in our cause early on and let us borrow money with nothing more than good faith as collateral. I met Aaron Jones, a lumberman from Oregon at our first convention in Spokane. Aaron liked what we were doing, and asked if he could help financially. When I told him a loan of $10,000 would be a huge help, he wrote us a check on the spot."

"Leonard Sargeant and Otto Teller loaned the organization a quarter million each, and Wallace Pate kicked in almost a half a million to get the Robb Creek purchase off the ground. Robb Creek was a Montana ranch that was up for sale. Rather than see it gobbled up by developers and subdivided, the brand-new RMEF bought it and later transferred it to the Montana Department of Fish, Wildlife and Parks. Anheuser-Busch clinched the sale by loaning RMEF a half-million toward the purchase.

Now Robb Creek is preserved forever. Elk and other wildlife will use it as a winter refuge, never having to be displaced by urbanization and the encroachment of man.

There have been many Robb Creeks, thanks to RMEF, and there will be many more. The biggest purchase of all was a $10 million transaction north of Yellowstone Park. Because RMEF was instrumental in buying and transferring those private lands to government agencies, elk will forever have room to roam.

I expect you bought this book because you love elk. If you aren't a member of RMEF, you're missing out on a superb organization, four issues of BUGLE a year, WAPITI - a monthly newspaper, and great friendships. If you want to participate in this outstanding group, write for information now. When you join, plan on attending some of the fundraisers and conventions. If you attend a national convention, look me up and tell me a hunting tale. I haven't missed a convention yet, and I don't intend to miss any of them. I know a good bunch of folks when I see them.

NOTE: For information on the Rocky Mountain Elk Foundation, write RMEF, PO Box 8248, Missoula, MT 59807. (800-CALL ELK).

NEVER ON SUNDAYS

When I moved to Utah in 1960 to study forestry and wildlife, elk were not numerous and could be hunted only by drawing a tag in a lottery. Odds of drawing were poor, and those who did were considered local heroes.

The hunter success wasn't all that great, because Utah was mass-producing mule deer and had little interest in elk. Grass in the forests was essentially reserved for cattle, and the powerful livestock associations successfully supported that attitude.

Sometime after I had moved out of the state to work as a forester elsewhere, Utah allowed unlimited resident elk hunting. When I moved back to Utah as a wildlife biologist, I was eager to hunt elk. I purchased a tag and planned a hunt with Pete Anderson, a fellow employee who worked with the same federal agency that I did. Pete's Dad and brother would also accompany us on the hunt.

I should explain that Pete and his family were good Mormon folks, abiding by all the teachings of the church. One of those teachings is to keep the sabbath, which, translated to outdoorsmen, means no hunting and fishing on Sunday. That day was reserved only for church services and meetings.

I had no problem with that constraint. I'm not a Mormon, but many of my pals in Utah were Mormons. They are good people, and most of them are avid hunters.

We left for the hunt Friday afternoon. Pete's Dad drove, while Pete and I and his brother rode as passengers in a pickup truck carrying a cab-over camper. This was a standard hunting rig in the West.

As we were about to enter the forest, we were stopped at a roadblock. A forest ranger greeted us and informed us that the fire danger was high, and warned us to extinguish smoking materials properly.

Pete's Dad smiled at the ranger and said, "Shucks, I don't smoke, don't drink, don't chase women, and in fact don't know what the hell I'm livin' for."

The ranger burst out in laughter, and so did the rest of us. Pete's Dad had a dry sense of humor that kept us constantly smiling.

We set up camp along the edge of a meadow high in the mountains. I was a novice at elk hunting, and didn't know a thing about it. I'd hunted elk only once before, and that was in Colorado.

Several other camps were also around the meadow, and I noted that there was a camp practically every place that had good road access. Obviously we wouldn't be involved in a hunt offering solitude and backcountry ambiance.

On opening morning we hiked around the forest. I headed for the highest country I could find, which turned out to be timberline at about 10,500 feet. I saw no elk but plenty of hunters. In fact, it was impossible to NOT see hunters.

About a half hour before dark, a cow and a calf elk appeared in the timber. I was walking along an indistinct trail, and evidently the animals hadn't seen me. They ran directly toward me, and at a distance of about three yards the cow skidded to a halt in wide-eyed surprise. She stopped so quickly the calf thumped into her hindquarters and was bowled over.

The pair regained their wits and tore off through the forest. I stood there chuckling at the elk, and was totally unprepared when a bull's bugle challenge burst out of the timber. I didn't have a bugle call with me, and even if I did, I had no idea how to use it. Standing silently in the forest, I waited several minutes and heard something large moving in the woods.

Moments later the piercing bugle emanated from the trees, and I stood rooted to the spot, with my rifle ready. Ten minutes passed, then fifteen, and then it was dark. I never heard the bull again.

Returning to camp, I found my companions packing for home, in order to attend morning church services. It had been an interesting one-day hunt, and I wasn't able to return to the area again that season because of work commitments.

I spent plenty of nights wondering about that bull, and my imagination worked overtime. I had him figured as the bull of the mountain, a monster animal that would easily make the record book.

It's both frustrating and fun to fantasize about what might have happened if I had more days to hunt that area. As it was, I was unknowingly initiated into elk hunting, and from that year on I never missed a season. I never made many more one day hunts, either.

THE HUNT THAT COULD
HAVE BEEN PERFECT

Reeee Take!

Billy Stockton is not your average American. He was born 200 years too late. Billy should have been fighting Indians and chasing grizzly bears and wolves back around the days of the mountain men.

Raised in a cow camp along the Bighole River in Montana, Billy grew up running the West with his Dad, cowboying wherever they could find work. Their trail took them from Mexico to Canada, and places in between.

Billy settled in the Bighole country after marrying Susie, and makes a life by outfitting, trapping, and making custom cowboy boots and leather goods.

I met Billy around 1980, when Jack Atcheson arranged a bear hunt for me. It was a meeting I'd looked forward to for a long time, because Billy's reputation preceded him.

I'd first heard about him when I was hunting the Bighole country years ago. Stories about him abounded, from his love of getting into a saloon brawl, to wrestling with enraged bears, and to guiding hunters to some of the biggest bulls in Montana.

The Bighole Valley is a harsh land. Winters are bitter cold, with temperatures well below zero more often than not. Mosquitoes are a nuisance in the short weeks of summer.

Despite those negatives, the Bighole Valley has something it can be proud of.

Real people. Folks who live there are hardy. They flourish in the cold temperatures and deep snow. They're survivors, willing to accept whatever nature dishes out.

The Bighole is also a mecca for outdoorsmen. The famous salmonfly hatch in the legendary river beckons anglers from around the world, and superb hunting for elk, deer, and bears appeals to hunters, some of whom hire outfitters, and some of whom hunt on their own. Moose live in the rugged forests surrounding the valley, and mountain goats inhabit the rocks that lie tight along snow-capped peaks.

Billy's house is a place that has a special charm. As Billy puts it, "you can throw a cat through the cracks in the walls."

It is an old building, heated only by a single woodstove in the living room. If the fire goes out, the house freezes, as simple as that. If Billy or Susie leave for a few days in the winter, they must hire a housesitter to keep the fires burning.

Deep scratches on the front door show where a wolverine once tried to get in, and it's not uncommon to see a bear from the kitchen window. More than once a bear has visited and raided the chicken coop.

Susie's kitchen is large, with plenty of room for her to work magic on the stoves. She feeds a dozen or more hunters during the peak of the season, and no one leaves the table hungry.

A few years ago, an archery manufacturer wanted to shoot an elk hunting video showing his products in use. He asked me to arrange a hunt with an outfitter for seven hunters and a two-man camera crew.

Billy was my first choice, and we put together a program. We'd hunt in mid-September, just right for elk bugling.

There was an interesting problem, however. I hadn't picked up my bow for three years, and I wasted no time practicing. I shot for at least a half hour every day, until I could consistently punch a paper plate at 30 yards.

When our crew arrived, we headed for a tent camp high in the mountains. Bow season would start the next day.

As luck would have it, one of the hunters hit a dandy bull on the opener. He and his guide tracked it, but darkness closed in and they gave it up. The next day they caught up to the bull, and the hunter nicely dispatched it with a second arrow. The elk had massive antlers, with six points on each very long beam.

Unfortunately, the cameraman wasn't with the hunter. He was with me, and I hadn't yet gotten close to a bull, though there was plenty of bugling going on.

Billy was my guide. I wanted him to get all the exposure he could, and since he was the outfitter and I was the hunter on camera, it was only natural that we hunt together.

Snow fell on the third day. It piled deep, and we were happy hunters. Unfortunately, the weather warmed, the snow started melting, and it turned the bulls off.

By the fifth day, Billy and I were discouraged. It was tough enough to work a bull given their lack of cooperation, and doubly tough to call one within range and record the shot on camera. We figured it was impossible.

Sometimes, however, the impossible happens. In this case it almost happened.

Billy and I were driving through the forest, almost aimlessly. We had exhausted all our options, and we had no idea how to get me and the camera crew on a bull. The cameraman couldn't travel very fast, having had open-heart surgery prior to the hunt, and he had heavy gear to move. He and his assistant, to put it simply, were not at all mobile enough to follow Billy and I as required.

As we drove, with the cameraman and his assistant following behind in their truck, we spotted a cow and calf moose feeding next to the road. We stopped for awhile to let the cameraman take some photos.

Billy and I sat in the pickup, perplexed and frustrated, when the bull bugled. We both looked up to see a bull and a bunch of cows skylined on a ridge about 500 yards away. The elk knew we were there, but they didn't seem overly concerned. Perhaps they were accustomed to seeing loggers in the woods.

We quickly alerted the camera crew, and when the elk moved out of sight, Billy started the truck and we headed down the road. Billy figured on driving a ways, parking the rigs, and then sneaking up on the ridge. We didn't go after the elk right then because we wanted them to hear us drive away. It would be best to leave the woods undisturbed.

Rather than wait for the camera crew to ready their gear and make the slow hike up the mountain, Billy and I headed up at a trot. We wanted to get things figured out. It was necessary to position the camera crew and me just right, considering the light and shade. Of course, the bull was the main actor, and we had to try to predict his moves, that is, if he was still around by the time we got to the ridgetop.

Billy and I eased up to the ridge, but the bull was gone. We heard him farther up the mountain in thick timber, where he'd moved his cows.

It seemed as if luck was going to be all bad, as usual, but just then we heard the faint bugle of another bull. We looked to see the animal on a distant ridge. He was so far that when he bugled, it would take a second or two for the sound to reach us. That might seem like an outrageous exaggeration, but it's the truth. I'll never forget it.

Billy blew a bugle challenge, and the bull answered. Suddenly the elk started moving, heading in our direction.

"I can't believe it," Billy said. "He's comin'."

"He can't be," I answered. "He's at least a half mile away."

We watched for a few more seconds as the bull traveled through a clearcut. He was darned sure coming for us, bugling as he ran.

"Quick, go get the camera crew," Billy said. "Hustle 'em up here, but be quick. That bull is hot."

I ran down the slope, and met the crew making their way up. I blurted out the situation, grabbed some gear, and hiked back up to the ridge.

Billy was almost beside himself when we got to the top.

"Hurry!", he exclaimed. "That crazy bull is right below us. He ran right straight over, and he's mad. He's down in the draw, thrashing the heck out of a bush."

We heard the bull plainly. He was whining and carrying on, and we could hear the foliage being ripped apart as he tore into the bush.

"Quick, get set up," Billy said. "I'll call for you, but I'll stay about 50 yards above you. When the bull comes, move so you can intercept him. He'll be headin' for me, and he won't know you're around. The wind is perfect."

I nocked an arrow and moved off down the slope, with the camera crew following.

"I'm going to position myself between Billy and the bull," I said to

Billy and I are happy hunters, but the video cameraman was a little sad.

the cameraman. "The slope is steep, so I might have to make a move at the last minute in order to see the elk. Watch what I do and stay with me."

There was a grassy opening in the ambush area. I set up, and heard the bull coming. The camera crew was above me, well concealed in a fallen tree.

Damn. I was too high. The elk would pass below me out of sight. My set up was no good.

I eased down the slope about 10 yards, intent on the bull. The camera crew was keying on my movements; I had no time to look back up or give them instructions.

Taking a position in the shade at the edge of the meadow, I waited for the bull. My heart was pounding, and I was shaking. This was my first bow hunt for elk, and it might as well have been the first hunt of my life.

Suddenly I saw the tips of his antlers as he marched up into view. I drew the bowstring and held the arrow in full-draw position. The bull would be very close, and the light was perfect. He was in the middle of the sunlit meadow.

The elk continued, and he never saw me in the shadows. I looked through the sight and saw his vital zone behind all four pins. I estimated him at 15 feet.

The arrow took him just behind the shoulder. At the hit, the bull snapped his head around and looked squarely at me. Then he ran off and disappeared around the bend of the slope.

For a moment I'd forgotten about the camera crew. I was too intent on the elk. I turned to smile at them, but they weren't in sight. I couldn't believe it.

The crew showed up moments later. They hadn't moved from their original position, and got nothing on film. So close but yet so far.

Billy rushed over, and we followed the blood trail. It was frothy, which indicated a hit in the lungs. Billy hadn't seen me or the bull when I shot, since Billy was out of sight as he called over the ridgetop.

The bull had gone only 60 yards. He'd collapsed and slid down the slope, landing in the middle of an old logging road. He carried five points to the side, and was in good shape.

It was with a great deal of emotion when I posed with the bull. Taking him with a bow was an incredible accomplishment for me. Not being much of an archer, I was amazed that it had all worked out.

I wasn't terribly upset at the camera crew's absence, though we were all disappointed. It was just one of those quirky things. The video was never completed. The company had required a good hit on camera, and we didn't get it.

When I think of all my elk hunts, the one with Billy is at the top of the list. I haven't given up my rifle for a bow, but now I can truly appreciate the difficulties and challenges of pursuing elk with archery gear.

Billy and I talk about the hunt a lot, going over each detail. One of these days I'm going to pick up my bow again and head out with Billy in his beloved Bighole Valley. And the next time there won't be any video team around.

To heck with the cameras.

THE HUNT I'D RATHER FORGET

"I wonder if elk are attracted to powerlines."

If a person hunts long enough he or she will sooner or later go on a hunt or two that they don't care to remember. The following story is about one of those. In order to protect the guilty, I'll give the outfitter a fictitious name. In order to protect the innocent, I'll do the same for my companions.

I was invited on an elk hunt by a high ranking official in the hunting industry. He had also invited several other people in his company.

Since the official (who I shall call Bill), had left it up to someone else in his corporation to line up the hunt, he relied on that person to arrange the trip with a reputable outfitter. None of us knew the name of the outfitter until a couple of weeks before the hunt.

I first became suspicious when the outfitter (who I will call Jack) arrived more than an hour late to pick us up at the airport. Most outfitters are on time, but Jack seemed to be a pretty affable guy, so I figured he was just running a little late, which can easily happen to a busy outfitter.

On the way to the hunting area, we stopped at a cafe for lunch, and Jack informed us that this wasn't going to be quite the wilderness trip as Bill had intended.

Jack explained that something had gone wrong with getting horses into his backcountry camp. However, Jack explained that we were set up in a good area and it would be a good hunt, regardless. We would still use horses, but the new camp would be accessible via four-wheel drive vehicles.

Being the nice guy that he was, Bill took the news in good humor. I should mention that Bill had been on only one other elk hunt. One other member of our six-man party had limited elk hunting experience, and none of the other members had ever been elk hunting.

When learning about the change in plans, my suspicions returned. There was something about Jack's personality that bothered me. Also some of the things he said about elk hunting didn't ring true in my way of thinking, and I began wondering about his experience as an outfitter.

I had met Bill and the other hunters at the airport by driving there with my pickup and camp trailer. I'd used the camper as a home base from which to photograph elk prior to the hunt. It was late September, prime time for photographing and hunting elk during the bugle season.

After lunch, we continued driving to the hunting unit. In addition to Jack and our hunting party, one of the guides (who I will call Jake) traveled with us.

We drove for a couple hours, and Jack turned off the highway onto a service road underneath a huge utility line.

Jack instructed me to park my camper next to the highway along the right-of-way road because the road was too rough for the camp trailer. Besides, I wouldn't need the camper since we'd be hunting out of Jack's camp.

After dropping off the unit, we drove along the power lines for about three miles. Finally Jack pulled off into an area that had several brand-new wall tents set up. They were within three yards of the powerlines.

When Jack got out of the truck and said, "This is elk camp," I grew more uneasy with his credibility. A river that was too deep to cross ran north of camp, and the south side of the powerline was hilly with heavy vegetation and brush.

The first item on our camp agenda was to assign tents to hunters. I was paired up with Bill and another hunter. The tent was really designed for two people, but we nonetheless arranged our gear as best we could and took the tent's small size in stride.

Once we were settled, we had dinner, which admittedly was very good. Jack also had some top-dollar libations that he generously offered to all of us, which is rare in any hunting camp. Typically, hunters bring their own refreshments.

After we ate, Jack informed us that there was no latrine at camp. We were to simply find ourselves a spot and make nature calls wherever we wished. This was a first in any elk camp I'd ever been in, and indicated to me that Jack was not only inexperienced, but had probably set up camp in a hurry.

When I asked Jack where the horses were, he said a wrangler was bringing them in that afternoon. That made me feel a bit better. Having horses, we could get away from the power lines and hunt the forests south of camp.

Jack also told us that the wrangler would be one of the guides. The guides would include Jack, Jake, and the wrangler (who I'll call Pete).

About an hour before dark, Pete arrived with about a dozen horses. He had parked his horse trailer near my camper and led the horses into camp.

When Pete climbed off his horse and walked into camp, he looked at our group and asked who the outfitter was. This was a most enlightening discovery, and the plot soon thickened.

Jack shook Pete's hand and told him to put the horses in the corral, which was a skimpy pole affair lashed to a bunch of trees behind camp.

I noted with serious concern that neither Jack nor Jake helped Pete with the horses. I later learned that Jack and Jake knew absolutely nothing about horses.

Jack told us that wake-up would be at 6:00 in the morning. Very interesting. In my opinion, we should have been in the saddles long before six.

At that point, I was expecting the worst. Since I was a guest on this trip, I didn't feel comfortable mentioning my fears to Bill who was paying for the hunt. In fact, I didn't say anything at all until several days later when Bill asked my opinion.

I heard Pete saddling the horses long before wake-up, and when we went to the tent for breakfast, I noted that Jack and Jake had barely awakened and made no effort to help Pete. Pete worked throughout breakfast by himself while Jack sat in the cook tent with his feet up, making small talk. Jake did the same.

Bill had indicated that he wanted us to trade guides and hunting partners so that we'd get the opportunity to know each other.

I was relieved to learn that another hunter and I had been assigned to Pete, who was a lean, tough, cowboy. I guessed correctly that he had plenty of woods sense.

The three of us rode out of camp at 7:30 in the morning and headed up an old road that led into the hills away from the power lines.

Pete scratched his head, grinned, and looked at me and said, "Guess this is as good as anyplace to start. Let's go see what this country looks like."

"I take it you've never been here," I said to Pete.

"First time," he replied. "I sure apologize for this, but we'll hunt as hard as we can and make the best out of this mess."

We had ridden about half a mile and stopped to take our coats off. The sun was rising and it was warming rapidly.

Pete pulled his horse up next to mine, and said, "You had much experience elk hunting?"

"Yup," I said.

"Then I guess you realize we were about three hours late getting out of camp this morning."

"Yup," I responded.

"We'll see what we can do to fix that for the rest of the hunt," Pete said, "but I don't think the outfitter and his guide know anything about horses. I'll try my best to get them saddled as quickly as I can."

"I'll help you, Pete," I replied, "I've got horses at home."

We rode around the hills that day looking for elk sign and basically scouting brand new country. We saw no sign at all and returned to camp around dark.

Jack wanted to know why we were so late getting in. He and Jake and the other hunters had gotten back to camp about an hour before dark.

By now the handwriting was on the wall. I had Jack figured out as a phoney, a bogus outfitter who should have never been outfitting for elk. My feelings were especially confirmed when I learned that Jake had ridden up the power line with his two hunters and had tied their horses to the edge of the power line about a mile from camp. There, the trio had spent the day, sitting under the power line, waiting for elk to show up.

The fact that no elk in his right mind would appear in that right-of-way on a warm balmy day hadn't occurred to Jake. Also, the deep, wide and swift running river adjacent to the power line made the right-of-way an unbelievably poor place to watch. There was no reason for elk to show. The place was a poor feeding spot, and elk probably wouldn't use it to cross.

Jack, on the other hand, had indeed heard a bull elk bugle. He and his two hunters had ridden down the power line, crossed the highway where my camper was parked, and heard an elk within a quarter of a mile from the highway.

Instead of working the bull by getting as close to him as possible in the timber, Jack tried calling near the highway. Of course, the bull would have nothing of it, and the day was uneventful.

The next day was a repeat of the first. Even though I helped Pete with the horses, Jack insisted on leaving camp after daylight. Again I said nothing.

I rode out again with Pete and a different hunter. We traveled all day in the mountains, but our efforts were uneventful. We couldn't locate any elk tracks, droppings, or rubs on trees.

Upon returning to camp, we learned Jake had pulled his same routine of sitting on the power line. One of his hunters grew impatient and took a walk in the hills. No one in the party saw anything.

Jack had again returned to the same place where he had heard the bull the first day, and this time, an elk bugled from heavy brush along the river. Sitting along the power line, Jack tried calling to the bull, but again the elk refused to advance.

When I heard this in camp that night, I realized that Jack was doing several things wrong. The biggest mistake was not being in that area well before daylight and determining the bull's location by listening to him bugle when it was still dark. The second major mistake was bugling from well-traveled roads near human traffic. Even a novice should have been aware of these basic strategies, but Jack had no idea that he was hunting wrong. He knew nothing about elk behavior and had no business being an elk outfitter. Unfortunately, Bill was paying him a handsome fee.

The next morning, all of us headed for the area that Jack had been hunting. By now it was obvious that Jack was not willing to leave camp at dark. I suspected that he was afraid to ride horses at night.

We were just 200 yards from my camper when we heard the bull bugle from the mountainside. With binoculars, we saw a good bull with a number of cows. He was fully in the rut, tending and herding his cows in a small group.

A few minutes later, the herd of elk walked into the timber and that was it. We spread out in small groups and tried circling the area the elk had disappeared into. The plan was predictably uneventful. We neither saw nor heard any elk for the rest of the day.

Over dinner that night, I made a casual comment that it would be a great idea to leave camp before daylight in the morning. I also suggested that another possibility might be for some of us to stay in my camper which was literally in sight of the elusive bulls.

Jack declined the ideas and said we'd continue hunting as we were. So much for my suggestions. I was still trying to be courteous, but was immensely frustrated. As far as I was concerned, that bull should have been meat on the table.

The sun was well up the next morning by the time we rode past my camper. This time a bull bugled in the same place we'd seen him the day before, and another bull bugled near the river. Jack sent two parties up the mountain for the first bull, while he and I and Bill tried to figure a plan for the bull by the river. I had the elk pegged in timber across the river and suggested we cross the highway bridge and ride along a trail that Jack thought ran along the other side of the river. He had heard about the trail secondhand, but since he'd never been in that country before, wasn't sure of its existence.

Indeed there was a trail. We rode along it to a point short of where we thought the bull had been, tied our horses, and sneaked along the river.

I tried bugling, but got no response. I wasn't surprised. It was late in the morning and the bull was probably wise to calls, or he might have been a herd bull, reluctant to meet our challenge.

After another hour of calling, we walked along the trail and located the spot where the bull had been. He had thrashed a dozen saplings into oblivion, and by the looks of the sign, had evidently been there for some time.

We spent the rest of the day exploring the timber along the river, but saw and heard nothing.

The next morning, Jack and Jake took two groups of hunters back to the river, while Pete and I and another hunter decided to ride to the end of the power line in the other direction.

This was a brand new area, and we found that the power line crossed the river and we could go no farther. However, we spotted an old road, probably made by seismic crews, that headed straight up the mountain.

We opted to go up it to look over new country, but it was such a steep, brutal, climb that we had to lead our horses rather than ride them.

Once on top, we discovered what we were looking for all along. The forest was laced with meadows and thick stands of evergreen timber. Elk sign was everywhere, and our hopes were renewed.

At one point, we were riding down an old road, and saw three cows cross in front of us. By that time it was getting late in the day, but we tried stillhunting until shooting light was over. We didn't see any elk, but we were enthusiastic.

Maybe we could be magicians and pull a bull elk, instead of a rabbit, out of the hat.

When we told Jack about our find that night at dinner, he admitted that he'd never been on top of the mountain, which was no surprise to me. In fact, Jack had never been in that area before we arrived except for a short deer hunt the week before. Curiously, Jack seemed a bit irritated that we had found a new spot that held promise on our own.

At dinner, we learned that Jack had taken one of the hunters on the trail that he and Bill and I had ridden the day before, but they didn't locate any elk.

The hunter confided in us in our tent later that when it started getting dark, Jack became frightened and foolishly rode out on the trail at a gallop, totally disregarding the hunter. The trail wound about through sharp snags, heavy trees, and rocky, brushy terrain. The hunter bumped his knee badly on a tree, and it was fortunate that neither of them were more seriously injured.

Jack decided to take Bill and another hunter back to the river while Pete, Jake, and the rest of us would head up the steep road into the new country we had found. Jake was assigned to be my guide, and I was underwhelmed, but I intended to make the best of it.

When Jake looked at the terribly steep road and learned that we'd have to walk up it, he immediately balked. He told us to go ahead with Pete, and said he'd spend the day at the top of the road where he'd wait for us until we'd return. Good riddance, I thought to myself as we left Jake in the rear.

When we got to the top, it was obvious that Pete had too many hunters. I suggested that I go off by myself. Pete agreed, and I slipped into the timber alone.

What happened next was an experience I'll never forget. I was walking along an old trail, and heard a swishing sound in the brush. I stopped and looked, and saw a bull elk walking directly toward me.

The brush was too thick to size up his antlers. He was in a dense tangle where you could only see part of the animal at a given time. I could barely make out movement atop his head as he walked, indicating the presence of antlers.

I immediately got down on all fours and crawled into a small bunch of spruce trees, shouldering my rifle and listening as the elk continued to walk straight toward me.

Suddenly I saw movement about 10 yards away. The elk appeared and I saw a small part of the antler. The bull looked big, and even though I had a clear shot at his chest, I couldn't shoot. There was an antler restriction in the unit we hunted and I had to positively identify my target.

The bull took two or three more steps and walked within almost five yards of me. It was a maddening moment. I could see his black legs, the lower half of his body, but still no antlers.

The animal stopped and remained motionless. All I could do was sit and watch and hopefully count those tines.

Suddenly the bull lowered his head, looked directly at me, and in the same split second bolted away in the brush. In that millimeter of a second, I saw his big rack and I was sure he was a legal bull.

Quickly I blew my cow call, and the bull answered with a series of grunts. I stayed where I was and blew the cow call again. The bull responded once more, and I could just picture him standing there, confused by the cow call. In the past, I had stopped bulls with the cow call even when they'd seen or smelled me, so I wasn't surprised by his hesitation.

The only thing I could do was move and find a vantage point where I could try to spot the bull. I slipped out of the spruce pocket, and eased up on the higher ground. The bull grunted again, this time about 50 yards farther away. He was in a low pocket of timber, and I had the advantage of elevation, but I still couldn't see him.

We played the game for the next half hour, but the bull stayed just below me and slightly ahead. My cow call seemed to calm the animal, but I still couldn't see him. Finally, he walked out of hearing and disappeared for good.

I hunted the rest of the day bugling, cow calling, and stillhunting, but never saw or heard another elk. I returned to the meeting place about dark and was almost reluctant to report my tale of woe, figuring my companions might think I made it up. Some outdoor writers have been known to do so for the sake of a story.

When I told them about it, Bill said he admired my patience. Another hunter might have shot the bull and then checked to see if it was legal. That kind of behavior isn't typical among hunters, but some unscrupulous people have done it in the past.

Bill's kind words made me feel better, but didn't relieve the total frustration I'd had at being so close to the bull and being unable to see him. Although we had one more day to hunt, I knew deep down that the bull would be my only opportunity at taking an elk.

My pessimism was right on target. We hunted the same area the next day, but nothing doing.

I never expect any elk hunt, no matter where or when, to yield an animal. I'm always grateful for the opportunity whatever the circumstances. In this case however, I was disappointed that we were outrageously bilked by a fraud who posed as an outfitter.

We could have lived with the sizzling powerlines overhead, the crowded tents, and the lack of the latrine. But the outfitter's negligence in not hunting the prime time of the day, as well as not knowing the country, was inexcusable. Jack and Jake's lack of knowledge in the elk woods was also unacceptable.

It was a learning experience for all of us. Those kinds of hunts unfortunately happen, and I was sorry to see Bill and his party set up by this outfitter.

The only bright side of the hunt was the fact that the outfitter is no longer in business. He said to heck with elk hunting. And I'm glad he did.

THE BULL THAT SHOULD HAVE STAYED HOME

Do it again...only this time make it sound like a real elk!

The Selway Wilderness in Idaho is one of my favorite places to hunt elk. It's a vast, rugged area that lies in the eastern part of the state, not quite in the Panhandle, and not quite in central Idaho.

The mountains are steep, and in most spots are densely forested with spruce, fir, and lodgepole pine. In some places ponderosa pines grow sparsely, with good visibility over the grass that grows beneath the scattered trees.

For some reason, all of my Selway hunts have been in the nasty, heavily timbered areas, where great jagged rocks thrust upward from the mountain tops. In addition, rain has been a big part of my Selway trips as well, turning the abundant huckleberry brush into giant sponges that defy state-of-the-art raingear.

My first Selway hunt was with Bruce Scott, a guide who had a pleasant disposition and a willingness to work hard. Included in the party was Vin Sparano, Executive Editor of OUTDOOR LIFE magazine, and his 18-year-old son, Matt.

This was my second elk hunt with Vin, and I'd hoped that it would make up for the first, in which he didn't get an elk, and which is another chapter in this book. It was Matt's first western hunt, and so between Vin and Matt, there were a couple reasons to see plenty of elk.

Our hunt was during the third week of September, just right for bugling. The area we hunted was one of the few in the state where rifle hunting was allowed during the elk rut. Several states allow September firearms hunting only in wilderness or backcountry units. Otherwise, gun hunts are opened in mid-October and early November, long after the bugle season is over.

Vin and Matt flew in to Missoula, Montana, where I picked them up at the airport. I was pleased at Matt's excitement at being in the West, remembering my own feelings long ago when I'd gotten my first look at the Rockies.

We checked into a motel in Missoula that night, and in the morning drove south into the lovely Bitterroot Valley, and then west over Lolo Pass and along the Lochsa River where we turned away from the drainage and toward the trailhead.

Bruce was ready for us with pack animals, and soon we were on the trail to camp. It was a pleasant 15-mile ride. As always, Vin loved every minute of it, and Matt seemed just as excited.

The camp was nestled in a group of evergreen trees. Vin, Matt, and I would share one tent, while Bruce, another guide, and the cook slept in another. The mess tent was a big, well-stocked affair, and I had a feeling we wouldn't be going to bed hungry during our stay.

Long before daybreak we were saddled up and ready to go. Bruce and I headed off in one direction, while Vin, Matt, and their guide went in another.

Bruce and I rode for an hour, then dismounted and tied our horses to trees. We eased up a mountain slope, listening for bugling activity. So far it had been strangely quiet. We hadn't heard a peep since we left camp.

It was around midmorning when we heard a bugle in the distance. The bull was a long way off, and we never heard him again to pinpoint his location.

Around noon, Bruce and I sat high on a ridgetop eating our lunch.

While we sat there, we heard large branches snapping in a patch of brush below us. I held my rifle ready, and after a half-hour vigil we spotted the cause of the disturbance. A big cow moose was walking through the thicket. She never saw us, and continued wandering about in the brush.

The moose was the only animal we saw that day. Fresh elk tracks were evident, but elk were elusive and shy. They were invisible in the evergreen forests and weren't at all vocal.

Several times Bruce and I looked at saplings thrashed by bull elk. By the height of the fresh scars, I had no doubts about the size of the bulls working the area.

Bruce told me about a giant bull he'd seen a week ago, during the first hunt. His client was unable to see the bull and never got a shot. Bruce lamented that the hunter simply couldn't see game. The huge bull offered a good target, but the shadows in the forest prevented the novice hunter from seeing the animal.

When we returned to camp that evening, Bruce pointed to a small clearing about 200 yards away. Ben Shultz, a veteran hunter from Eugene, Oregon, had taken a fine six-point bull at the spot during the first hunt. I've since met Ben, and he's everything I'd heard him to be. He's taken 43 elk in a lifetime of hunting, and is still at it, even though he's in his 70's.

Vin and Matt hadn't seen anything that first day, but there was enough sign to keep our enthusiasm high. Only a few hunters had been in the area the first week, and the area was so large that many of the drainages hadn't been visited by a human.

Rain fell that night, and we headed out under cloudy skies. It was more of the same. Lots of horseback riding, walking, and climbing. We heard no elk, and none responded to our calls.

Day three was a repeat of the first two. The lack of vocalization was puzzling. Elk were around us, but they all had good cases of lockjaw.

A blanket of snow greeted us when we awoke the fourth morning, but much of it melted by noon. An inch or so clung to the forest floor in shaded areas. We had located a few tracks in the snow, but the warm weather erased the betraying snow too early to do any good.

Around midafternoon, Bruce and I eased to the bottom of a steep drainage. The forest was fairly thick, with a mix of pine and fir trees.

At one point, I spotted a unique snag that had caught the sunlight just right. It would make a perfect backdrop for a photo.

"Stand by that snag and put the bugle call to your mouth," I said to Bruce. "That's a great spot for a picture."

Bruce obliged, but the pose didn't look right.

I pose with the elk who charged us. He should have stayed put.

"Let's try it again," I said, "but this time really blow the call. It'll look real with your cheeks puffed up."

Bruce blew the call and I snapped his picture, but I'd hardly pressed the shutter button when we were startled by a screaming response from a bull elk. He was no farther than 75 yards away.

We couldn't believe it. For four days we'd bugled in some of the Selway's prime country without an answer, and here we were, fooling with a camera when a bull responds.

I quickly grabbed my rifle, exchanging it for the camera. The bull was on us instantly, whining and carrying on behind some brush just 15 yards away. All I could see was his black legs. The undergrowth hid his body.

Suddenly the bull turned and ran off. I still couldn't see him.

"Blow the call again," I whispered to Bruce. "Hurry".

Bruce called again, and the bull reacted immediately. This time he showed up about 125 yards away, but I saw his chest through the trees. I'd have to thread the needle and put the bullet between a bunch of pines, but I didn't have a choice.

I steadied the Winchester Model 70 against a tree, drew a careful bead, and fired. The bull staggered at the report, and lurched ahead about a yard.

Though he'd changed positions, I had another good view of his chest. The second bullet thumped him solidly, but he continued standing.

I put a third bullet in him, and that was it. The elk fell heavily to the ground with three rounds into his chest.

He was a dandy bull, with six points to the side and long tines coming off thick beams.

After dressing him, I walked over to where he'd been when Bruce initially bugled. I was amazed at the sign. There was no doubt that the bull had himself a little home in the forest. His lair had plenty of grass, and a small spring provided a good supply of water.

The elk had reacted predictably. Even though Bruce and I called into the drainage from the top of the ridge two days straight, the bull wouldn't respond. We had to accidentally stumble close to his lair to get him to answer.

The snag was indirectly responsible for me getting the bull. If we hadn't made the call at that spot, we'd have walked off and never known the bull was around.

As I climbed back out of the drainage that night, I wondered how many other bulls we'd passed within close range. From that point on I started calling much more aggressively when I hunted during the rut.

Now I call at least once every 15 minutes and leave well-traveled trails far behind. I'm convinced that it's essential to get right into a bull's back yard before he's agitated enough to answer.

I learned something else interesting on that hunt. Because it was getting dark and we had a long hike to the horses as well as a long ride to camp, we didn't do any skinning on the elk. All we did was pull his entrails and open him up so he'd cool.

Normally I'll skin the neck where the hide is extremely thick and covered with very dense fur. I'll also cut the windpipe away because it will quickly sour the meat around it.

This time, however, I left the neck intact because I wanted to photograph the bull in the morning when the light was better. One of the requirements of being a hunting writer, unfortunately, is taking plenty of good pictures.

There was some snow on the ground a few feet from the carcass, so we tugged on the bull so he'd lay on the snow. Then Bruce and I double-timed it up the mountain through the heavy timber. We

Bruce Scott looks over the Selway from a ridgetop.

reached the horses by nightfall, and took another two hours to ride to camp.

Vin was all eyes and ears when we got to camp and I decided to play a little joke on him.

"What'd you shoot, Zumbo," he asked when Bruce and I walked into the cook tent. "We heard the shots and I bet Matt that you killed a big old bull. You're the luckiest doggoned hunter I ever met."

"Sorry to disappoint you," I said. "I got a fair three-point muley. Just a so-so deer."

I tried to keep a straight face and asked the cook if we could eat the deer's heart for dinner. He agreed, so I left the tent to retrieve the big old bull's heart, which, of course, is about three times bigger than a deer's.

I pulled the heart out of the saddlebag and brought it into the tent.

Vin looked at it and I watched in amusement as his facial expression changed immediately from nonchalance to total enlightenment.

"You (bleeping) bum!" he said. "I should have known you wouldn't shoot a so-so deer in elk country."

Vin's expression changed again. "How big?" he asked.

"One of my best ever," I said. "Six to the side, and wide with long beams."

There was a lot of backslapping, and I must admit we had a small toddy to celebrate the bull. As I cooked the heart, I told Vin about the circumstances of the kill. If it wasn't for that unique snag, the bull would have stayed home.

As it turned out, neither Vin or Matt got an elk. It was perhaps the strangest behavior I'd ever experienced during the rut. Animals just weren't vocalizing. They were all around us, but they were almost impossible to see in the dense timber.

When Bruce, the cook, and I went back the next morning to pack out the bull, I was amazed that the neck meat was still warm, even though it was lying on the snow. The rest of the animal was cooled nicely.

I was lucky and managed to salvage the neck, but in a few more hours it would have been soured. It was a good lesson, and I was glad I didn't have to lose good meat to learn it.

I learned lots of things on that hunt. One of them is to never give up, no matter how bad it looks, and never to assume there are no bulls around because you don't hear them.. You might have to get close to their front or back yard to entice an answer. And most importantly, don't say to heck with elk hunting until the last minute of the last day.

THE LAST HITCHHIKER

I knew my first outfitted hunt was going to be a great success. I was so sure, in fact, that I'd laboriously constructed a huge meat box to fit in my truck. The box was well insulated, and big enough to hold four elk quarters.

Because of some unfortunate occurrences that might embarrass the outfitter, I'll call him Harry, which isn't his real name.

I drove to Harry's home, and the plan was to spend a night at his house and then we'd head for the trailhead the next day with packhorses and gear. Besides Harry and me, we'd be accompanied by a wrangler, two guides, and another hunter. Harry would do the cooking, and the hunter and I would each have a guide.

Harry insisted that we have a cool one at a local bar that first evening, so the other hunter and I obliged. The local tavern was jumping. Hunting season was in full swing, and locals and outsiders alike were trading lies in the saloon.

Though we tried to convince Harry to leave early, he'd have none of it. Finally we managed to carry him home, but only after he'd drank himself silly.

The next morning, to my surprise, Harry was in great spirits and apparently unaffected by the previous nights' bout in the bar.

He told me before we left his house that elk camp would be dry, and he apologized for his behavior the night before. There'd be no drinking for him and the wrangler and guides, but he said I was free to bring whatever I wanted. I declined, and was pleased that alcohol wouldn't be a problem. I was beginning to have serious doubts.

We were packed and in the saddles by noon the next day. Camp was 15 miles up the trail, nestled high in a wilderness area, just under rocky snow-capped peaks that mountain goats lived on.

My guide, who I'll call Mike, and I hiked into several basins the first day, but we saw no elk. Fresh sign was uncommon, but we knew elk were in the country.

It was more of the same the next day. Mike and I hunted hard, walking and hiking at least 10 miles, but still we hadn't come across any elk.

Harry's meals were superb, and I couldn't complain about Mike's guiding ability. He seemed to be tuned in to elk, and we did a lot of sneaking through timber, glassing, and working into secluded drainages that might hold elk.

The weather had been very warm, and we all talked about snow. If the weather would cooperate, we might have a chance at an elk.

The other hunter and I shared a tent. He was from back east, and he was having the time of his life, even though he hadn't seen an elk, either.

"Just being here in the magnificent Rockies is good enough for me," he told me one evening. "I don't care if I get an elk or not."

I knew exactly how he felt, because I too am a former Easterner. I had the same awe for the western mountains. They never grew old.

Snow never came, and we didn't see an elk. Harry suggested we leave camp and hunt another area. The guides agreed it would be a good move.

The new spot was fairly accessible from town, so the other hunter and I stayed at Harry's house.

Leaving camp was a mistake. Not only did we see no elk, but we couldn't keep Harry out of the bars. Every night several of us literally carried Harry home. His house was just down the highway a couple hundred yards from the saloon.

I went home with an unpunched tag and an empty meat box. I can't say it was Harry's fault. We hunted good country every day, but it just wasn't in the cards to kill a bull.

I left Harry's house at daybreak. It was 5 degrees below zero when I started for home, and I'd driven about 30 miles when I saw a hitchhiker standing along the highway.

Feeling badly for him in the bitter subzero cold, I stopped and picked him up. He looked okay — a big bearded guy carrying a full backpack with camp gear and a sleeping bag.

He got in my rig, which was a Dodge Ramcharger (same style as a Ford Bronco or Chevy Blazer), and he immediately made a sarcastic comment about the condition of my vehicle, which was full of hunting gear. I thought the guy had a dry sense of humor, so I let it pass.

A bit of small talk revealed he was from eastern Canada, and he was headed to Southern California to find some wild women and drugs.

I should have thrown him out of my rig at that point, but I continued driving down the road.

"What's in there?" he asked, when he spotted my guncase.

"A rifle."

"What're you doing with a gun?"

"I've been elk hunting"

"What's an elk?"

"A big animal, bigger than a deer," I responded. I was not liking this guy at all, and wasn't interested in conversation any longer.

"You mean like those cows?," he said, pointing to some cattle along the highway.

"Yeah."

"Let's shoot a cow."

"Are you crazy?"

"Nah. If you're chicken, gimmie the gun. I'll shoot one."

"Don't touch that gun!" I said. I turned to him and gave him the meanest sneer I could muster. My teeth were clenched and he knew I was mad. He kept his mouth shut for awhile.

Finally he said he was sleepy, and asked if he could stretch out in the back of the rig. This guy was a looney, and I was intending on dumping him off at the next gas station, but I told him to get some sleep.

He untied his sleeping bag and rolled it out. It looked like a good bag.

"What kind of bag is that?" I asked.

"I dunno."

"You don't know what brand it is or what it's made of?"

"How should I know? Some truck driver picked me up yesterday. He stole a credit card from a guy, and me and the trucker had us one hell of a shopping spree with the card last night. That's how I got the bag and all this other stuff."

At that the man crawled into the sleeping bag and was fast asleep. That was too much. I wanted the guy out of my rig immediately, but it might not be that easy. He was big, obviously a thief, possibly a felon on the run from the police, and he might be carrying a gun or a knife.

It happened that I had a .41 Magnum Ruger revolver lying next to my seat on the floor of the rig. I unholstered the revolver, placed it in my hand between my side and the door, and pulled over to the side of the road.

"Get out!" I said to the hitchhiker.

"Where are we," he said.

"In the middle of nowhere," I answered. "Get out now."

"I think I'll stay. I ain't gettin' out" he said. Then I saw a strange look come over his face, and I knew instantly that this person was dangerous.

"I think you'll want to, pal," I answered, and I slowly raised the big .41 Mag and pointed it between his eyes.

"Hey, man," he said, "I'll go. Don't shoot me."

"Just get out easy and slow," I said.

I couldn't believe this was happening. I had never pointed a gun at a human before, but I knew that in this case it was necessary. I don't think the man understood anything else.

The hitchhiker got out with his gear, and when his feet hit the ground, he started running. I watched with satisfaction as heavily falling snow swirled around him and he disappeared in the whiteness.

I called the highway patrol from the next gas station, and reported the incident. They took my name and telephone number, but they never contacted me. I suppose all I could offer was hearsay, and I never knew what became of the hitchhiker.

I wish that was the end of the story, but Harry and Mike also had an incident with a gun, about three years after the hunt. They were drinking heavily in a bar, and they got into an argument.

Harry went home, got a gun, returned to the bar and shot Mike in the back. Today Mike is a paraplegic, relegated forever to a wheelchair. Harry served time in prison and is now out.

My hunt had a bizarre ending, and my outfitter and guide are living through nightmares. Sometimes life deals us some tough times.

I often wonder what would have happened if I hadn't had my .41 Mag handy. Maybe I would have had to have said to heck with elk hunting long before I ever really got started. I might not have had a choice. For sure, however, I said to heck with picking up hitchhikers from that day on.

SMELL YOUR WAY TO ELK

A number of years ago, I hunted elk in an area I'd long been enamored with. It was a mid-September hunt, just right for bugling. Two outfitters ran the hunt. They were from outside elk country, and had just purchased the outfit a couple years before my hunt. They were a couple of good guys, but they weren't terribly knowledgeable about elk hunting. They'd made money as businessmen elsewhere, and looked to outfitting as a fun way to retire. They quickly learned that retirement and outfitting don't go hand in hand. In fact, they are no longer in the hunting business.

When I hunted with them, I was amazed at the number of clients in camp. There were 16 of us, which was twice as large as any other camp I'd ever been in.

As I soon learned, the outfitters had booked about 90 hunters, which was about 30 more than normal. Extra guides had to be hired at the last minute, and additional facilities constructed at camp to accommodate the hunters.

The strategy was to gather up all the hunters after breakfast, ride in a single group to a patch of timber, and put each hunter on stand while the guides rode horseback or walked through the forest, trying to drive elk out to the standers.

With the exception of a small bull that ran to a stander, the plan was a dismal failure. That was no surprise to me, because trying to drive elk is often an exercise in futility. Sometimes it works; more often than not, it doesn't.

Since it was prime bugling season, I wondered why the outfitters weren't interested in calling. I asked one of them while we were standing around a fire during a snowstorm. I'll never forget his answer.

"Bugling doesn't work," he said. "Elk have changed their ways. Bugling is a waste of time."

"Are you serious?" I asked. "You're kidding, of course."

"I'm dead serious," he responded. "It's a waste."

I looked for a glimmer of a smile or a grin, but the man was truly serious. I couldn't believe it.

"I don't agree with your opinion," I said politely. "Would it be okay if I hunted alone the rest of the week. I'd like to try bugling."

The man had no problem with that, but because of liability laws and Forest Service regulations, a hunter who was booked with an outfitter had to be accompanied by a licensed guide working for the outfitter. That meant I was stuck with the frustrating mode of hunting we were involved in.

Apparently the outfitter had talked to his partner at dinner that evening. The partner called me aside and said I was welcome to try bugling with one of his guides.

I assured the man that I didn't want to be a pest, or to complicate the hunt. I'd go along with whatever they'd planned, and he renewed the offer to hunt with the guide.

The next day was one of the most enlightening I'd ever spent in elk country. My guide demonstrated something so unbelievable that I've never written about it before, because I figured no one would believe it. This is the first time it ever appeared in print.

I'll call my guide Sam.

Sam used his nose to find elk. I don't mean smelling a bunch of elk when you're 100 yards or so downwind. I can do that. I mean smelling them a quarter to a half mile away, and precisely pinpointing their location.

We had ridden about three miles out of camp when Sam suddenly halted his horse and held up his hand for me to stop.

"I smell something," he said, "but it's not an elk."

I was skeptical, but sat quietly in the saddle.

Sam sniffed the air, and directed his horse through underbrush. "We're getting close," he whispered.

I was totally amazed when we rode 10 yards further and looked at a stump ripped apart by a bear. Fresh snow had fallen during the night; the bear's tracks were red hot.

"I don't believe it," I said.

Sam grinned and said nothing. We continued riding through the forest.

I tried figuring his trick, just as you try to decipher a magician's act. There was no way Sam could have been tipped off to the bear's presence. The brush was too heavy to have seen the bear, and the animal's tracks came in and left the stump from the opposite direction we'd ridden in on.

An hour later, we rode through heavy timber, and I heard a branch pop to our right. It was a loud noise, and only a large animal could have made it. Another branch cracked, and another.

Sam kept riding, looking straight ahead. I'd been watching him; he never turned his head to look toward the sound.

"Sam," I said in a half whisper, "don't you hear that?"

"Yeah," he said, "but it's only a moose. I smelled it."

I stood up in the stirrups, looking in the direction of the sound. A moose was easing away from us through the forest.

I'm sure Sam hadn't seen the moose. The first branch cracked when we topped a knoll, and Sam's head never varied from looking straight ahead. The moose was off to our right at a sharp angle. This guy either had one heck of a gift of smell, or he was clairvoyant. I was dumbfounded.

Later in the day, we were hiking through a timbered jungle. Sam suddenly stopped at one point, and sniffed the air.

"Elk," he said, "but they're a long way off."

"How far?" I asked.

"At least a quarter mile," he answered.

We moved upwind, with Sam sniffing the air every now and then. Moving silently in the brush was impossible, but elk are noisy themselves and will often allow you to approach closely if they don't see or smell you.

Finally, Sam stopped.

"They're close," he said. "Get ready".

He'd no sooner spoken when there was an explosion in the timber. Sam was a couple yards ahead of me and up on a log, where visibility was a bit better. I couldn't see what was crashing through the forest.

They were gone in seconds, but I had no opportunity for a shot.

"Two bulls," Sam said. "A raghorn and a spike"

"Are you for real?" I asked. "You tracked those bulls to their beds by smelling them."

"All in a day's work," Sam said with a smile. "Let's see if we can dog 'em again, but we need to let 'em settle down first."

While we paused, Sam told me his Dad, who was one of the oldest outfitters in the state, also had the ability to ferret elk out by smelling them. Sam told me there was no trick to it; he just paid attention to what his nose told him. He also said you couldn't do it if you smoked, or if you had a bad cold. A keen nose requires a healthy body.

Soon we headed off, and Sam worked the mountain thermals. We made our way through the timber until he was positioned correctly with the breeze. Then we started our hound dog routine.

A half hour later, Sam stopped and raised his hand. He muttered something under his breath, walked a few more yards, and suddenly waved me forward.

"Hurry," he said. "Get up on a stump or log. Those elk are close."

Too late. The words were barely out of Sam's mouth when the elk flushed from dense cover. Again they escaped unseen. We investigated their tracks; it appeared they were the same two bulls we'd spotted earlier.

We ate lunch, and were about finished when a bull bugled. Sam bugled back, and the bull charged close, but we couldn't see him. The elk turned, ran straight away from us, and bugled as he ran.

Sam bugled again, and the bull ran along several ridgelines. He bugled every 15 seconds or so, and seemed mighty worked up.

"That raghorn is upset," Sam said. "He's hot, but he doesn't want to fight."

When Sam tried another call, the bull charged in again. I saw a flash in the timber, and the bull ran forward several yards. He was behind some brush, and I could see his dark legs, but that was all.

The elk stood there momentarily, and bolted away, staying behind cover as he ran. We heard him bugle as he went, and finally his screams disappeared into the distance. That was the last we saw or heard of the bulls that day.

Sam had other guide commitments the rest of the hunt. The other guides with the big group of hunters were planning some huge drives and needed Sam's help.

I didn't get an elk that trip, but I had observed one of the most incredible hunting feats in a lifetime of hunting. Sam had an amazing talent, and I hope you believe my account of the hunt. I wouldn't blame you if you said to heck with this book because you think I'm fibbing, but Sam's story is true. You meet all kinds of characters in the elk woods.

WHICH BULL DO I SHOOT?

Com' on, we'll go get ya a good'n!

Jim Baker and I hiked up the wooded slope long before dawn. Elk bugled everywhere; it was impossible to tell how many there were. I'm not exaggerating when I say that perhaps 10 bulls were bugling within hearing distance.

I was hunting on the famed Vermejo Park in northern New Mexico. The park has been synonymous with big bulls, and has been described in many magazine articles.

Vermejo Park isn't a park at all, but an enormous ranch that, at the time I hunted it, sprawled over more than 400,000 acres. Owned by Pennzoil Company, the ranch includes benchlands with pinyons and junipers, as well as beautiful spruce fir forests high in the alpine zones, where huge mountains tower over the land.

Gary Wolfe was the ranch manager when I hunted Vermejo, and Jim was his assistant. Gary is now an officer with the Rocky Mountain Elk Foundation in Missoula, Montana. Jim Baker took Gary's job at Vermejo, and is still in charge of hunting.

I was in the middle of writing my hardcover book, HUNT ELK, when I arranged my Vermejo hunt with Gary. I had never hunted one of the southwest ranches, and I believe that first-hand experience is required in order to have credibility as an author.

Gary gave me a briefing about hunting the ranch when I arrived, and showed me to very comfortable quarters. My accommodations were hardly what you'd expect in an elk camp. I would be living in a lovely lodge nestled at about 9,000 feet. I had my own room, as did each of the other hunters, and I felt quite pampered.

Jim Baker was my guide, and we visited by the fireplace the night before the hunt.

"Are you looking for a really big bull, or a good, mature animal," he asked.

"A big guy," I answered. "As big as we can find."

"You willing to hunt hard?" he said.

"I'll do whatever it takes," was my answer.

"Good." he said. "If you'll trust me, we'll find a heck of a bull. We'll be looking at lots of elk; just don't lose your cool until we see the right one."

I liked Baker's attitude. This would be truly a trophy hunt, and I knew I'd be passing up good bulls until Mr. Big came by. I hoped I was up to the task of waiting. It's tough to let good bulls go by, but I knew I was hunting a very special place.

We were hunting the first season of the fall, and it's called the Trophy Hunt in Vermejo's literature. It didn't take long to find out why.

When shooting light approached, we moved on a bull that sounded worked up. He was bugling frequently, and he was close.

Jim and I eased toward him, and by the time we sneaked through the forest, shooting light had arrived.

The bull appeared in the forest about 80 yards away. He had a bunch of cows, and I immediately liked his antlers. The elk carried six points to each antler, and he was as pretty a bull as I could have wanted.

I rested my rifle on a stump, and was about to sight through the scope when Jim realized I was going to shoot. He hadn't seen me position myself for the shot.

"No," he whispered. "Don't shoot. We can do better."

"You're kidding," I said. "That's a dandy bull."

"I asked you to trust me last night," he responded. "Honest, we can find a better bull."

I had mixed feelings as I watched the bull move off through the timber. Seeing a bigger bull seemed a bit ambitious, but I was willing to give it a try.

By nightfall we'd looked at a dozen more bulls, none of them better than the first we'd seen. I was beginning to have doubts about passing on the big bull.

These Vermejo guides are putting in a good day's work.

Back at the lodge, we'd learned that a father-son team had taken their elk. The boy had killed a dandy, but Dad apparently shot the wrong animal, which was nevertheless a decent bull.

As the man recounted it, several bulls were running single file, and the guide told the hunter which animal to shoot. Either the guide was wrong, or the hunter had not counted correctly. Either way, one of the smaller bulls in the herd was claimed by the bullet. Even at that, the bull was a six-pointer.

Jim and I looked over a number of bulls the next day, but none was outstanding. Other than the first morning, I still hadn't readied my rifle for a shot.

One of the other hunters in the lodge had taken a fine six-point elk that day. The bull had been drinking out of a waterhole when the hunter and his guide had rounded a bend in their vehicle. The hunter, who was in poor physical condition, got out of the truck and killed the bull.

Jim had received a tip about a big bull from some loggers who were cutting timber on the ranch. They'd seen the elk high in a meadow, and they said he was a beauty, with seven points on each side.

Jim didn't have to ask me twice if I wanted to try for the bull. I was ready.

The next morning, we hiked through the forest toward the clearing, and by shooting light we were at a good vantage point. While we climbed, we heard several bulls bugle from the direction of the meadow.

As the gray of pre-dawn slipped away and the landscape brightened, I was able to see animals moving in the clearing. I didn't count them, but there were at least 50 cows and calves.

Suddenly a bull walked into the small slot of view that I'd been looking into. He was no doubt the big boy, but I couldn't move. Two cows were peering up at me, and had me spotted.

Worse, the bull was directly behind a small spruce tree about 15 yards in front of my position. I was pinned. If I moved, the cows would spook, and if they didn't, the small spruce had the bull's chest perfectly blocked.

It was a frustrating dilemma. I sat there for 10 minutes, and finally the cows moved on. For some reason, the bull stood rooted to the spot, looking back up the mountain at something we couldn't see. The spruce tree was still in the way.

Jim was sitting behind me, and he tried a bugle call to move the bull.

It worked. The bull took a step, threw his head back, and bugled. My bullet was on its way instantly, drilling the big animal just behind the shoulder.

The bull stood there at the report, looking around in confusion. I quickly chambered another round, centered the crosshairs at the same spot, and saw a tiny red spot on his hide, exactly where I'd aimed.

He didn't know it, but the bull had been fatally struck. I shot again, and hit the elk almost at the same spot as the first round. This time the elk lurched forward, bugled, and ran 10 yards.

He was still on his feet, and I was able to keep him in sight, though I had to take a few steps to see him through the trees. I fired one more time, and the elk went down.

The bull was definitely worth the wait. He was the biggest elk I'd ever taken up to that time, scoring 333 Boone and Crockett points.

Interestingly enough, the famous actor Slim Pickens was at the Vermejo that week, hunting out of another lodge. He took a bull

*Vermejos bulls
are big and will
test any meatpole.*

the same day I got mine. Slim's bull was huge, scoring 378.

As I understand it, Slim's bull maintained a high enough score during the mandatory drying period to qualify for the Boone and Crockett record book. I don't think Slim had the bull entered in the book, however. The wonderful man passed away soon after the hunt.

In all my years of elk hunting, I've only had one elk mounted, and that's the one I took on the Vermejo. He isn't the biggest bull I've taken, but he brings back memories of a superb hunt in a beautiful spot.

Memories linger long after the aches are forgotten and the meat is consumed. That's a big part of hunting, and those reflections will always linger and remind me of a big bull in a pretty meadow. Those memories are one of the reasons I can't say to heck with elk hunting and really mean it.

THE SECRET SPRING

But we already been to bed...it's the first day of ELK SEASON!

If you hunt elk in dry country, the presence of water can be a great place to start looking for animals. Unfortunately, waterholes are seldom well-kept secrets. Hunters have a way of telling others where water is, and soon everyone is lurking around the oases.

When I worked as a wildlife biologist for the federal government, I was a rather unhappy boy. All we seemed to do was sit around the office, drink coffee, and do tons of paperwork that meant little or nothing to wildlife. As soon as our government agency got a huge desk project done, after thousands of hours going into it, someone in Washington would dream up a different way to do the paperwork, negating the millions of dollars spent on the initial project.

On a rare day, however, you really did something that meant something. One of those gems of satisfaction involved a small spring that seeped out of the ground at the base of a very arid, juniper-covered mountain.

Because of the spring, a very nice bunch of elk hung around the area. The tiny waterhole had no lush vegetation nearby to betray it, and it wasn't identified on topo maps.

Only a few people knew about it. They included a rancher whose cows drank from the spring, a few government employees with my agency, a few hunters, and, of course, me.

To our delight, we were given the go-ahead to improve the spring. The Washington bureaucrats had kicked loose several thousand dollars for the project.

The problem was with livestock. Cows trampled the spring so bad they actually closed it up by compressing the clay so heavily that the water was shut off. When that happened, usually in August when the animals needed it most, the cows and the elk had to go elsewhere.

Our objective was to modify the spring and keep it flowing all summer. We did it by digging down deep with a backhoe to unclog the spring, and piping the water to a trough. The whole area was fenced off to keep cows and elk out, but the trough was outside the fence so animals could drink from it. Excess water from the trough slopped out and created a wallow below for elk.

It was a great success. Livestock, elk and deer had plenty of water during the hot summer, and elk had a wallow to fool around in.

The region around the spring was in a limited-entry area. Only a few dozen tags were awarded in a lottery draw, and success was very high in the unit. Most hunters took their elk around well-known springs on a large mountain a half-dozen miles away from our secret waterhole.

I never drew a tag for the unit, though I tried every year, but a couple pals of mine drew tags. They had asked me where to apply, and I'd suggested the unit surrounding the spring. I also told them I'd take them hunting there if they drew, but if they ever told anyone about the spot I'd burn their houses down.

Now then, you might think that, as a government employee, I was being selfish and maybe unethical because the spring was on public land. In my defense, I saw the waterhole as a rare perk of being a federal employee, other than, of course, a pension, sick leave, medical insurance, and all that good stuff. To me, knowledge of a few places like the spring was a payoff for the frustrations of the desk job.

Furthermore, if I put the word out about the waterhole, a gazillion hunters would be hovering over it during the season. As I saw it, the secret would eventually leak out. Besides, there was no guarantee the elk would consistently use it.

My friends arrived the day before the season. I took them for a drive, and headed for the spring, which is adjacent to some juniper trees. Otherwise, the area is basically sagebrush and grass.

I drove across a deep wash, up the other side, and parked the truck in some junipers.

"What do you see up on that sagebrush flat, fellers?" I asked.

The hunters looked and looked, didn't say a word, and I knew they hadn't seen the 80-plus head of elk laying around in the sage.

"Where you looking?" one of them asked. "I don't see any—

"Good Lord!" the other hunter interrupted. "Lookit those elk! LOOKIT THOSE ELK! There must be about 150 of them."

"More like 83," I said. "There's a six-pointer and two spikes in the bunch. They've been hanging around all week. Let's hope other hunters haven't seen them."

I slowly turned the truck around, drove back across the wash, and headed for camp. I knew that the boys would have a tough time sleeping that night.

It was two o'clock in the morning when I heard noises. Both my friends were awake.

"Why don't you guys go to bed?" I said. "We gotta get up at four."

"We already been to bed," one of them said. "We just got up. It's opening day of elk season."

I groaned a great deal, and made a big fuss out of being rudely robbed of precious sleep, but I was secretly as excited as they were about the elk. Neither of my friends had killed an elk. If the herd would remain where it was, and no other hunters spotted them, my pals should have some shooting in a few hours.

Daylight was still an hour away when I parked the truck in the wash. We sneaked through some juniper trees, guiding ourselves by starlight, and I stopped about a half-mile from where the elk had been the day before.

"Let's wait ten minutes and listen for a bugle," I suggested. "If we hear one, we can locate the herd."

The words were hardly out of my mouth when a bull bugled. He was precisely where I figured he'd be.

I instructed my companions to slip ahead and belly-crawl as close to the elk as they could. There was no good way to approach. Every possibility involved sneaking through sagebrush that was low to the ground. It would be a tough stalk, and there was no sense for three of us to go. I'd wait in the junipers until I heard them shoot.

Shooting light had finally arrived when I heard a shot, followed by another.

Wonderful! Two shots, two bulls. We could drive right to them, have them dressed and loaded in a couple hours, and be back to camp long before the noon hour.

Then another shot rang out, and another, and another. It quickly became evident that something had gone bad wrong, because I counted the shots and knew my friends had emptied their rifles. I sprinted through the sage, and saw the hunters staring at the elk. The latter were beating it up the mountain; the former were looking mighty forlorn.

When I glassed the fleeing herd with binoculars, I noted with despair that all three bulls appeared quite healthy. It was not an encouraging sight.

I approached my pals, and they were looking at the ground, kicking at clods of dirt. "We missed," one of them said. He didn't have to say it, because I knew it, but it had to be said anyway.

"How far were they?" I asked.

"I don't know," my friend said. "I'd guess close to 400 yards."

We turned to look at the herd of elk that was in full sight. They were trotting up the open slope of the mountain.

"I think that crazy six-point bull is bugling at us," I said, as I watched them through binoculars. The elk had his mouth open, his head laid back, and his belly was rippling.

Sure enough, we heard the distant bugle seconds later, It took awhile for the sound to reach us, because the elk were easily 1,000 yards away.

When my friend pointed out to where the elk had been when they shot, I paced the distance. It was 225 yards.

They didn't ask how far, and I'm glad they didn't. I didn't want to hurt their feelings by telling the truth, and I didn't want to lie either.

I knew about an old road that climbed the mountain the elk ran up on. A half hour later we were on top of the mountain, and, of course, the elk were nowhere in sight.

The mountain was blanketed with thick forests of juniper. I figured the elk were holed up somewhere, and I had the feeling they hadn't gone very far.

"Let's look from this ledge," I suggested. "With that many elk in the bunch, maybe we can spot one."

Ten minutes had passed when one of my pals made an announcement.

"I see a cow," he said. "Down below us. She's just standing in the trees, nibbling on some brush.

Though we looked for 20 minutes, we couldn't see any other elk. The cow had bedded, and we could just barely see her rump.

"Try a stalk," I suggested. "Get the wind right and ease up through the junipers. You might move in close enough."

The plan worked better than I expected. I waited on the ledge, and I heard a shot an hour later. Seconds later I heard another shot, and all was quiet, except for a whooping sound in the trees. It sounded like my pals were doing a bit of celebrating.

As it turned out, one of the hunters sneaked within 100 yards of the edge of the herd. He spotted the big bull, but a cow was lying directly between the bull and the hunter. My pal waited 20 minutes, and when nothing happened, he whistled sharply. The cow jumped up to her feet, and my buddy drilled the bull instantly at the base of the chin. My other friend killed one of the spikes, and there were two mighty happy hunters on the mountain.

We were happy, that is, until it was time to pack the elk out. My truck was 600 yards straight up the mountain, and I couldn't drive any closer to the elk.

We quartered the animals and lugged them on our backs to the truck. Six hundred yards might not seem very far, but I can assure you it was an ordeal. It took us the rest of the day to get the meat to the truck.

The following year, another pal's wife drew a tag for the unit. I took them to the spring, which had a bunch of elk around it, but they were inconsistent. They'd be there for awhile; then they'd disappear.

The three of us were sneaking through the brush above the spring early opening morning. Shooting light had arrived, and I looked back at my friend and his wife.

"Okay, get ready," I said. "We're going to pop over this little knoll, and I'm going to say 'there they are', just like in the movies."

I was astounded when the elk were exactly where I said they'd be. My pal and his wife didn't know it, but I had only been kidding. Of course, I never told them any differently. I was plumb proud of myself.

Unfortunately, the elk had spotted us, and quickly ran up the mountain. I told the lady to shoot the big five point bull, which was the biggest in the herd, but her husband said it was too far. I'd figured the bull to be 250; he said 400 yards.

I know better than to get involved in a domestic squabble, so I shut my mouth. She didn't shoot, the elk got away, and that was that.

We tracked the elk and jumped them again in the junipers. She had another opportunity for a shot, but again her husband said it was too far. Again he'd estimated the bull at twice the distance I did.

It doesn't matter who was right. She didn't get an elk, but that's often the way it goes in the elk woods.

I was disappointed that she didn't get her bull, but I wasn't nearly as upset as I was when an interesting new regulation change was made years later by the Utah Division of Wildlife Resources. I had moved to Cody, Wyoming, and learned that Utah had just passed a law allowing nonresidents to apply for limited-entry units, which included the unit that held the spring.

I was a bona-fide nonresident of Utah at the time, but for some dumb reason I'd missed the application deadline. I was even more upset when I learned that the handful of tags for the unit were undersubscribed.

I couldn't believe it. For a good part of my adult life I'd been trying for a tag and couldn't get one. Then the state offered one on a silver platter and I didn't take advantage of the opportunity.

Did I try the next year for a tag? Of course. Did I get a tag? Absolutely not.

The nonresidents who got tags the first year all killed six-point bulls. They told a bunch of friends, all of whom applied the following year. From that point on, the tags have been oversubscribed every year.

I still try, though. I want to hunt that doggoned little spring before I say to heck with elk hunting.

WHEN GAMBLING PAYS OFF

In my frequent hunting seminars and lectures I always mention that statistics are against the elk hunter. If you average all the western states, you'll learn that four out of five hunters go home without an elk each year..

That's a pretty dismal figure, and there's not much the average hunter can do about it. Elk hunting is simply too unpredictable. The country is often mean and nasty, and the weather is often too nice. On public land, there are usually big crowds of hunters, and on private land, fees are commonly too high for the average Joe.

Is there a way to beat the odds other than going on a high dollar hunt to an exclusive ranch or with an expensive outfitter? You bet, and I mean that literally. Betting on an elk hunt is a great way to beat the odds.

Before you think I'm going loco, let me explain. Every western elk state offers special limited-entry hunts that require a lottery draw for a tag. Those hunts usually yield much better odds of taking an elk, and big bulls are a lot easier to come by. Here's why. In much of our elk country, animals are too consistently harvested because of the high hunter pressure. Mature bulls are few and far between, and few ever live long enough to grow the kinds of antlers that we dream about.

The limited entry hunt, on the other hand, has relatively few tags. Hunting is restricted, and a good proportion of animals usually escape the fall season. Furthermore, many of the special hunts are in lower elevations with good road access. In lots of places you can collect your bull almost from your vehicle.

A couple years ago, I drew a Colorado tag in a limited-entry unit. Unlike other states, Colorado offers a preference point if you don't draw a tag. The point is applied to your application the following year, and your chances of drawing are highly increased.

I had three points when I drew, and I really didn't want the tag that year, because I was scheduled to be elk hunting in Canada and couldn't make the first several days of the Colorado season.

At any rate, the computer smiled at my application. It was with bittersweet regard when I opened the envelope that held the tag. If the circumstances were different, I'd have been ecstatic. I'd drawn one of the very finest units in Colorado, with a hunter success rate of about 80 percent. Traditionally, the majority of bulls taken are five and six-pointers.

Most hunters would have been deliriously happy at such a dilemma. Having a top-rate Colorado and Canadian elk hunt at the same time would not be perceived as a problem by onlookers, and I received no sympathy from my pals.

I resolved to make the best of it, and went to Canada in good spirits. Because of a busy schedule that summer, I had been unable to properly scout the Colorado unit. As it was, I'd looked over a number of maps and made several phone calls to wildlife agencies. At least I had a starting place when I began my hunt.

With the Canada hunt over, I drove my pickup to Colorado on October 4th. The season had opened October 1st, and I'd missed the first four days of the hunt.

With a camp trailer full of food and a pickup truck full of gasoline, I arrived in the dark and parked the rig in a sagebrush flat. I had no idea what to expect in the morning, and was immensely frustrated. For years I'd anticipated drawing the tag, and I'd intended on scouting the area prior to the hunt and locating some big bulls.

I knew that even though there were comparatively few hunters in the unit, they'd have pushed the elk around by then. The surviving animals would be holed up tight in the meanest cover they could find.

The area was very low in elevation, around 4500 feet. That might seem quite high to some folks who live elsewhere, but in western Colorado that's about as low as you can get. The country was arid with lots of large sagebrush expanses and dense forests of juniper trees which grow about 10 to 20 feet high. Spooked elk would be deeply entrenched in the junipers.

I'd had plenty of experience hunting the juniper forests before, and they weren't any fun. The branches grow from the ground up, and they're laced with thick foliage. Visibility in the junipers is terrible. Invariably you'll spook elk long before you see them.

By first light I was in the truck, driving about the unit to become acquainted with the lay of the land. I wanted to look over the terrain and escape cover.

I talked to a few hunters who were about. Most had finished their hunts and had taken good bulls, but some were still looking. One of the locals told me that I'd have a tough time finding a branch-antlered bull. He said the easy ones were killed on the opener, and the escapees were dug deep in the junipers.

I spotted a spike and a few cows that day, and pretty much got a good look at the country. I hadn't been really hunting, just scouting the unit. When daybreak arrived in the morning, I'd be stillhunting and glassing areas where I'd found fresh sign.

I didn't see an elk the next day, but I wasn't the least bit worried. Every year plenty of good bulls survived the season, and I was confident I'd find one.

The next morning and afternoon was equally unproductive. With darkness coming on, I settled into a comfortable spot on a ledge where I could glass for miles below and around me. Sooner or later I'd see a bull.

About a half hour of light was left when I saw an animal lying in the junipers about 800 yards away. I put the binoculars down and unlimbered the spotting scope.

Through the lens I saw an elk with a light-colored hide. Bulls are normally much lighter colored than cows, and my suspicions were confirmed when the animal turned its head. All I could see was a part of an antler, but the bull looked interesting enough to warrant my full attention.

Fifteen minutes passed before the elk got up and moved toward a grassy spot to feed. I saw him intermittently in the trees, but I had a good enough look to know he wore six points to the side. The elk was most satisfying to me, but there was no way I could narrow the range before dark.

I watched him until I couldn't see any more, and carefully slipped away toward the truck. I'd be back in the morning.

My camp was in a nice little spot. A big cliff swooped down from the sky to the west, and tall sagebrush grew just east of camp. I sat around a little pungent fire flavored by sage branches and listened to the coyotes howl. As I watched the flames leaping toward the stars, I wondered what the bull elk was doing. Tomorrow would tell.

I parked the truck a long way from where I'd seen the bull, and used starlight to guide my way to the vantage point on the ledge. Once there, I made myself comfortable and watched with awe, as I always did, the birth of a new morning. The splendor of sunrise never grew old.

Slowly the grayness that precedes dawn illuminated the vista around me. Blurred shapes became forests and rock outcrops, and bit by bit I could see color washing into the landscape. Soon it would be shooting light.

The lovely vigil was shattered by the piercing scream of a bull elk. I literally jumped at the sudden violation of the quiet, and looked intently for the source of the sound. The bull sounded close, almost too close to be true.

Moments later an elk appeared in the brush below me. I strained to get a good look in the poor light, and saw that the animal was a cow. Presently another elk walked into view, and my binoculars helped me identify it as a bull, no doubt the same bull I'd seen the previous evening. He wasn't huge, but had six respectable points on each beam.

The bull was about 400 yards out, about as far as I cared to shoot. I didn't want to try calling for fear of driving him deep into the timber. A herd bull will commonly gather up his harem and run away from the sound of a challenging bull.

There was no way I could get closer, because I was on the ledge of the ridge. To make matters worse, two cows and a calf started walking away from me, and the bull stared at them. I knew he'd quickly follow, and he'd soon be out of range.

My 7mm Browning was up to the task of the long shot. I'd

practiced with it at very long ranges, and I was confident I could anchor the bull if I had a solid rest.

A rock in front of me provided good support for the rifle. I laid my cowboy hat on the rock, nestled the rifle snugly into the hat, and had as perfect a rest as you can want.

Shooting light had arrived and I was ready. With the scope centered a trifle high over the bull's shoulder, I carefully squeezed the trigger.

The elk dropped instantly at the shot, and I knew he'd never regain his feet. From the way he plunged to the ground, I suspected the bullet had broken his back.

It took me 20 minutes to ease off the ledge and down to the bull. My guess was correct. He was dead, with a shattered spinal column.

The bull would win no awards, but he was nonetheless a trophy to me. I took some photos of me and the bull by using the self-timer on the camera, and set about dressing the animal.

It was dark when I had him loaded in the truck, and I knew I'd put in a good day when I arrived at camp.

The gamble had paid off. I'd beaten the odds, thanks to the lottery system. The way I see it, you need all the help you can get in elk country. If you draw a tag for a limited-entry unit, you probably won't say to heck with elk hunting when you head out of the hills with an unpunched tag. Chances are you'll be hauling meat and antlers home. That's all you can ask.

WHEN THE RAIN WON'T GO AWAY

Remember he ain't a Roosevelt Elk until he crosses that highway!

Rain is always an important consideration when we hunt. Some places it doesn't rain much at all; in others it's a fact of life. I can tell you, from limited experience, that the west coast is one of those spots where you'd better figure on rain— lots of it.

I wanted to hunt a Roosevelt elk for a long time, and had the opportunity to do so in Washington. Roosevelts live in Oregon, Washington, and in British Columbia. Their habitat is a strip of forest — usually very dense and very wet forest, from the ocean to the crest of the Cascade Mountains, a range which runs from B.C. down into the states. There are a few Roosevelt elk in California, and a fair herd on Afognak and Raspberry Islands off the coast of Alaska.

A lady in Vancouver, Washington called me out of the blue one day and asked if I wanted to hunt elk near Mt. St. Helens. All I had to do, she said, was to agree to participate in the fundraising activities at Vancouver's Rocky Mountain Elk Foundation chapter banquet.

My involvement would be simply to agree to hunt with the person who was high bidder at the auction. The lady and her husband, Bert and Garry Day, would host me and the high bidder at their elk camp near Cougar, Washington. The town became famous when Mt. St. Helens blew its top in 1980.

I learned later that I wouldn't be technically hunting Roosevelt elk. The Boone and Crockett Club recognizes the subspecies in Washington only if the elk are living west of Interstate 5, which runs from B.C. down into California. Since Mt. St. Helens is east of I-5, I'd be after Rocky Mountain elk. Many biologists disagree with that delineation but it really didn't matter, because I wasn't figuring on shooting a candidate for the record book. My primary objective was to hunt the dense, rainy country of the northwest.

I got my wish. It had been raining for days prior to the hunt, which started in early November. Carl Phillips, who was high bidder, and I, were prepared for the worst.

Opening morning seemed even more rainy, but we headed out in good spirits. Garry drove us to the hunting area in his pickup, and when we reached the spot he'd selected, we immediately started hiking in the soaked forest.

The plan was to stillhunt slowly down to a grassy clearing that was in the bottom of a drainage. While we walked in the thick hemlocks, the rain was temporarily shut out by the thick canopies, but we were quickly wetted when we moved from the protection of the hemlocks.

Actually the rain wasn't all that bad. The temperature was in the 50's and the wind wasn't blowing. We all wore plenty of wool, and were reasonably comfortable.

We had been hunting for about two hours when we startled a cow and calf elk in the forest. They spooked immediately, and I was pleased to even see an elk.

This was a brand new experience for me. The forest was different from the Rockies, as were the hunting conditions. I began to understand why many hunters said that pursuing Roosevelt elk was a tough proposition. Indeed it was. These animals had to be hunted in nasty forests, often in miserable weather.

A couple hours later we reached the grassy spot, but there were other hunters around. I was amazed to see where one enterprising hunter had camped all night inside the burned out cavity of a huge tree. He had blocked the cavity with a piece of plastic to keep the rain out, and was just as snug as could be.

At one spot, we came to a stream where there shouldn't have been one. According to Garry, the heavy rains had created new temporary waterways.

The rest of the day was uneventful, and it was good to get back to

Rain is a fact of life in western Washington.

camp. Bert had prepared a delicious meal, and dry clothes lifted our spirits.

We learned that it had rained five inches that day. In another state that might have been mind-boggling, but in western Washington it was no big deal.

The next two days were uneventful, so we decided to switch areas and hunt with Ray Croswell, who is as avid a blacktail deer hunter as I've ever met. Ray is a friend of Garry's, and hunts elk now and then, but blacktails are his first love.

Garry and I split up, while Carl hunted with Ray. We didn't see any game that day, but Ray told us about some fresh sign he'd seen.

There was about a half hour of light left when Garry and I were walking out of the forest late the next day. We hadn't seen anything, though we'd located elk sign.

As we were walking down a trail, Garry and I were startled by a bunch of elk that had been rummaging around in the forest just in front of us. The animals, about 20 in all, crashed away through the dense underbrush when we blundered around a bend in the trail.

Garry and I ran after the elk, blowing our cow calls as we ran. The elk stopped immediately, and began vocalizing with us. Some of them chirped, some barked, and a bull bugled.

It was an unbelievable situation. The elk had seen us, but they were nonetheless confused by our actions.

Again the elk ran, and again we chased them and blew the calls. For the second time the herd stopped and answered.

I could see animals in the brush, but it was too dark to identify them. The timber was thick, and night was coming on.

The animals finally left. Garry and I couldn't help but laugh at the incident. We had been running like maniacs after the elk, and they lingered around, apparently not believing we were dangerous. Evidently the cow calls had them confused.

We were after the elk in full force the next day. Garry, Ray, Carl and I split up, stillhunting in the timber.

It was interesting country. Douglas firs, hemlocks, cedars, spruces and firs made up the forests, with thick underbrush, especially vine maple, blanketing the floor.

I heard a shot about 8 o'clock in the morning. I walked toward the area where the shot came from, and found Garry standing over a fat, four-point bull.

He hadn't shot the elk. It was Ray, who really wanted only a deer, who made the kill. Ray hit the bull solidly with his .270, and was following the blood trail when Garry spotted the elk lying on the ground.

Our buddy Ray also had an elk tag in his pocket, and even though he apologized profusely, he had a grin on his face as we skinned and quartered the bull. By the time it was dark, we had the elk quartered and lashed to backpacks. Ray was still apologizing when we finally made it down to the trucks.

I didn't feel at all sorry for him as he struggled with a quarter as well as the antlers and hide on his back. Some guys really know how to mess up a hunt, and the next time I hunt with Ray I intend to shoot the biggest blacktail buck in the forest.

I don't get mad. I just get even.

CUT HIM OFF AT THE PASS

Don't know about you...but I've had about all this fun I can stand!

I'm sure the sun shines in the Selway, but I've hardly seen it, despite more than 35 days of hunting this famous Idaho wilderness over the years.

The hunt with Jack Wemple was no exception. Rain fell heavily, though I must admit that the hunt was the shortest I'd ever had in the Selway.

Wemple is a top-flight outfitter who lives in Victor, Montana. He hunts both Idaho and Montana, and when he's not in the boonies, he's running an excellent guide school out of his Montana lodge.

Wemple runs a tough school. When the students are done, they know about shoeing horses, packing and caping game, wrangling horses, and coping with the whims of hunters.

Jack and I, his wife Shirley, and guides and hunters headed for his

My Selway bull just wouldn't shut up, allowing us to cut him off at the pass.

wilderness camp the day before elk season. The horseback ride in was nice, until my horse was stung by a hornet as we passed the buzzing nest along the trail.

I should explain that a horse stung by a hornet is mighty upset, almost always lunging, bolting, and carrying about like a maniac. That's why I was almost decapitated. Lucky for me the branch wasn't six inches lower on the tree as my horse steamed through the woods. All I got was a nasty bump. Of course my horse was the only one stung.

Opening morning was drizzly and overcast, but Jack and I left camp in high spirits. We rode a half dozen miles, tied our horses to trees, and descended into a place fondly known as Jack's hole. This was a nasty place rife with soggy, dense huck bushes overtopped with thick spruce and fir trees. Jack said it always held a super-duper bull, which was good enough for me. I'm always a sucker for a super-duper bull.

We slid and fell to the bottom, sometimes on all fours, and sometimes upright. It was beginning to be fun, until I thought of the climb back out. Then it wasn't fun anymore, and I couldn't wait for Jack to call a halt to the rapid plunge to the seemingly bottomless abyss.

Mercifully, a bull bugled from Lord knows where, putting a stop to our rapid descent. The sound bounced around in the horribly wet brush and trees, and we had no idea as to the elk's location.

Jack bugled back and the elk responded. This time we got a fix on his location, but only that he was somewhere within a quarter mile or so in the miserable thicket.

We played games with the bull for an hour, but he stayed put. Finally he moved away, until his bugle was a faint squeal in the distance.

I guessed he was a herd bull. Looking back at the situation, I'll wager I could have persuaded him to come in with a cow call, but that was long before anyone tried fooling with cow calls.

It took us three hours to climb back to the top. The rain hadn't quit, but it was almost comfortable as we sweated and strained in our slow hike up.

"We'll find a bull in the beddin' grounds," Wemple announced, as we ate a sandwich on top of the ridge.

"What's the beddin' grounds?" I asked. I thought I knew a little something about elk, and always figured they bedded where they happened to choose after a night's feeding. I never knew they had a specific 'beddin' grounds.

"There's a grassy slope under some scattered trees that the elk like to loaf in during the day," he explained. "It's just a mile walk over there, and it's worth a try."

We walked the mile, and soon were slipping about in the 'beddin' grounds. We hadn't gone 300 yards when I saw a bull elk staring at us.

"Bull elk," I whispered to Jack. "He's standing under that tree."

Jack looked, and we glassed him with binoculars at the same time.

"Five points," I said, "do you think we can do better?"

"I'd pass," he said, "but you do what you want. There are bigger bulls in here."

My brain rapidly accessed the situation. He was a nice five point bull, and he might be the only branch-antlered bull I'd see.

I raised my rifle, centered the scope's reticule squarely on his chest,

Jack Wemple rides down a Selway trail from the area where we ambushed the bull.

and lowered the rifle. The bull made an about face, almost on cue, and fled out of the country.

"That might have been one of the biggest all-time mistakes I ever made on an elk hunt," I said to Jack. "Maybe I'm an idiot."

"I think you did the right thing," he said. "Maybe we'll find his grandpa."

For a couple hours we wandered about, and heard a bull bugle across a canyon. He was a long way off, but there was still three hours of light left.

We decided to move in on him, and started down a steep slope where we'd have to hit bottom, cross a river, and hike up the other side.

As we were sliding down the mountain, another bull bugled, this time above us on the slope we were on. Jack and I stopped and listened.

This bull was worked up bad. He'd bugle a bit, but mostly he'd whine. It was almost a nonstop whine, which other hunters and writers often call a grunt.

For a full minute we listened to the bull keep up his constant squeals. Jack and I decided he was worth looking at and gave up on the bull across the canyon. This guy on our slope was acting nutty, and we might be able to home in on him if he kept it up.

We listened for a few seconds more, and determined that he was walking along a contour from left to right. If we could hurry up the mountain and intercept his path, we might intercept him. In order to keep him pinpointed, though, he had to keep whining. We banked on that, and started up the slope as fast as we could.

The searing pain in my lungs and terrible ache in my legs were salved by the sounds of that crazy bull. Somehow Jack and I kept sprinting up the steep mountain. The bull kept up his talk, and we maintained our forced march. It was a supreme test, but the bull kept my adrenaline flowing so good that I wasn't about to slow down.

Somehow we gained the elevation we wanted, but the bull shut up. He was close the last time we heard him, but now we had no idea where he was.

Jack and I were creeping the last 50 yards. He stood up once to look and suddenly he dropped to the forest floor like he was hit by a falling log.

"The bull is right there!" he said. "RIGHT THERE! Stand up and shoot him."

I stood, and saw a great six-point elk staring at me 20 yards away. I snapped my rifle up the same moment he lunged, and fired at a blur of motion. For a fleeting instant I thought I'd missed, but I knew he was down in the thick brush.

Jack and I ran over, and found the bull dead. He was a beauty, with six long tines attached to each thick beam.

The ambush had worked perfectly. It was the first time I'd ever heard a bull vocalize constantly, and we soon learned why.

As we looked over the animal, we saw a nasty hole high on the bull's snout, almost between his eyes. At first we couldn't figure it out, but then we realized that the bull had apparently been in a fight with another bull, and had been badly gored. He was mad at the world, which explained his lack of cows as well as his continual whining.

There was a bit of daylight left, but I'd carelessly forgotten my film in the tent. Jack managed to fish a roll out of his backpack, and I was readying my flash equipment when suddenly the sun appeared over a cleft in the clouds and beamed straight onto the fallen elk.

We hurried some poses, and as soon as Jack shot the roll, the clouds closed in and it remained overcast for the rest of the week.

I can't explain why that happened, but then, there's lots of things I can't explain about elk hunting. Maybe that's one of the reasons why I love it so much.

A BULL FOR JUDI

Shoot!   Shoot!   Shoot!

The scene before me was as wild as any I'd ever experienced in a lifetime of hunting. My 19-year-old daughter, Judi, raced along the creek on her madly galloping horse, closely following outfitter Everett Peterson, whose charging horse was just a length ahead of Judi's. I followed close behind the two, and I was mighty upset.

We were literally trying to cut off a big bull elk at the pass, but I was afraid the bull would disappear before Judi could dismount.

"Get off the horse and shoot," I screamed loudly, trying to be heard above the clatter of hooves. "Judi, get off the horse NOW!" I repeated.

Unbeknown to me because I couldn't hear, Everett urged Judi to stay on longer to close the distance between her and the elk.

The bull was running full bore down the mountain slope to our right, trying to cross the creek we were paralleling to gain safety in the timber on our left. Once crossing the creek, he had to run 300 yards across an open sagebrush slope to make it to the trees, and I knew he could cover that ground in a matter of seconds.

Finally Everett jumped off his horse. Judi did likewise, in a swift, fluid, motion, and I was momentarily pleased that all her rodeoing since she was eight had paid off. My daughter knew about horses.

Quickly she jerked her rifle from the scabbard, and ran up behind Everett and I.

"No time to find a rest," I said. "Take a kneeling position and shoot when you're ready."

The bull was now half way across the sagebrush, but Judi didn't fire.

"I don't want to shoot when he's running," she said in a panicky voice. "Blow your cow call, Daddy!"

It wasn't a request, it was an order, and I was shocked into action. I was so caught up in the crazy circus that I'd completely forgotten the call, and I was amazed that Judi had the presence of mind to remember it. Even if I'd remembered it, I wouldn't have tried the call. Why should it work? The bull was acutely aware of our presence; we were in the open, and our horses were prancing nervously.

What happened next was so amazing that I wouldn't repeat it if I didn't have witnesses. No one would believe it.

I blew the cow call, and the bull stopped instantly from about 175 yards out, staring at us as if he was seeing us for the first time.

Judi fired, but the .270 bullet was high, striking over the bull's back.

The elk lunged forward, and I blew the call again, this time with more volume. Incredibly, he stopped and stared at us again.

Judi's second shot was also high, and she was getting rattled.

"Where are you holding?" I asked excitedly.

"Over his back, Daddy. He's a long way away," she answered.

"No, he's not," I said firmly. "This time hold right on his chest. Calm down, and make believe you're shooting at a paper target."

At the third shot, the bull faltered slightly and I heard the solid thump of the bullet striking flesh. He crashed ahead in the direction of the timber, and I blew the call once more.

I was even more astounded than before. Though he was hit, the elk stopped again, allowing Judi another opportunity.

She waited too long to shoot. The elk ran into the forest, disappearing for good. I could see the concern on Judi's face. She had no idea as to the bullet's effect.

"You hit him good," I said. "I think you've got yourself a bull elk, honey."

"But suppose he's not hit good," she stammered.

"We'll find him," I said firmly, "but first we'll eat lunch."

"Lunch? Let's go look for the bull right now," she said. I saw her eyes moisten, and big tears slid down her pretty face.

I explained why it was necessary to give the elk at least a half hour's rest. It wasn't to let him lie down and stiffen up and die, which is an old wives tale, but to allow him to bed close by, allowing us to sneak up and administer a finishing shot if necessary.

Judi couldn't eat her lunch, and I wasn't doing very well myself. It occurred to me that we might not find the bull. If that happened, all the years I'd spent teaching Judi to hunt might have been in vain. I was afraid she might give up hunting if she wounded an animal.

We were hunting with Everett Peterson, a long-time outfitter who hunts mule deer and elk in the magnificent Wyoming Range in the Bridger-Teton National Forest of western Wyoming. Also in our party was Judi's fiance, Matt Inkster.

I'd intended to take Judi and Matt elk hunting in Wyoming by myself, but Everett changed my mind. A week before the elk hunt, I'd hunted mule deer with Everett and his son in law, Lynn Madsen. Lynn was just starting into Everett's outfitting business, and I took a good four-point muley buck on the hunt, after passing up a dozen other mature bucks.

"Why don't you bring Judi and Matt elk hunting here?" Everett asked as I was leaving deer camp. "I've got extra bunks and I won't be busy. I can show you some country for a couple days, and a bunch of elk too."

It didn't take much convincing. Judi and Matt attend the University of Wyoming at Laramie, and they had only two days to hunt. If anybody could put us into elk quickly, I knew Everett could. The veteran hunter is a charter member of the Wyoming Outfitter's Association, and had guided many notable hunters over the years, including Jack O'Connor.

And I liked Everett. A tough Westerner who was raised in Wyoming, he has a gentle way about him. There is always a smile etched into his rugged face and a twinkle in his eyes. He is the kind of man you like to be around.

The elk season started on Sunday, which happened to be Homecoming Weekend at the University. Since Judi and Matt play the trumpet in the band, they had to perform at the Saturday Football Game. I drove to Laramie, photographed her and Matt as they marched in a parade, and sat with them in the band section during the first half of the game. As soon as they finished the half-time parade on the field, we rushed out of the stadium and headed

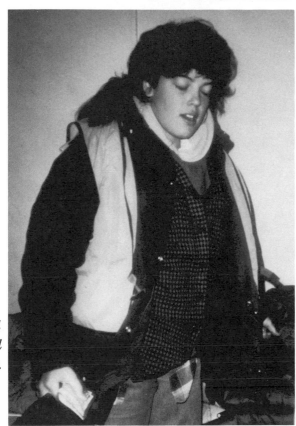

Judi is plumb tuckered out, and learns the hard way about elk hunting.

for Everett's camp, which was 200 miles away. Judi and Matt gave up homecoming weekend fun to go elk hunting, but neither of them had second thoughts. It helped, too, that their band director allowed them to leave the game after halftime activities. The fact that he himself is an avid hunter no doubt affected his generosity.

We pulled into camp at 10:30 at night. Everett greeted us, and showed us to our tent. Judi, Matt, and I crawled into sleeping bags, and it didn't take much for me to fall asleep. It had been a crazy day. At noon I was in the midst of screaming, wild football fans, and after driving across most of the state, I was now in a quiet elk camp where coyotes provided the only music.

We'd been in the saddles two hours by the time the sky started to brighten in the morning. Everett wanted to be at a particular spot by shooting light.

Judi and Everett chat about the prospects of finding bull elk.

We finally dismounted, tied up our horses, and hiked along the mountain for a half mile. Everett told us to sit and get comfortable.

Matt took a position about 20 yards away, and I sat with Judi. I had an elk tag, but didn't have my rifle. This was Judi and Matt's hunt.

According to Everett, undisturbed elk consistently traveled along the mountain slope across from us on opening morning. It was a reliable spot, one that hadn't failed him in years.

We sat for more than an hour, but nothing happened. Everett shook his head, and slipped over to our position, suggesting we wait another half hour and then ride farther up the mountain. He explained that if elk didn't show soon after shooting light, they probably wouldn't appear at all.

A few minutes later I looked over to see an elk walking slowly through the trees. There were a few very small clearings, the largest as big as my pickup truck.

Three cows and a pair of calves walked into view, feeding slowly. Then a small bull stepped out, but Judi was sitting two feet to my left and couldn't see his antlers.

Frantically I pointed out the bull, but she wasn't sure enough to shoot, since three or four other elk were partially visible in the trees. Matt couldn't see the bull, either.

The bull finally walked into the timber, and that was the last we saw of him.

After a one hour vigil, Everett got up and suggested we walk to our horses and ride higher. I was the last to leave, and before turning around a bend, looked across the mountain for one last look.

To my surprise, another herd of elk was crossing through the trees, and by the time I signaled our party it was too late. One of the animals had a very light pelt, which usually identifies a bull, but I never saw antlers.

To make our morning even more frustrating, Matt looked high up the mountain and spotted a good bull and two cows walking through the firs. They were too far for a shot, and we watched them top out over the ridge and disappear.

The rest of the day was spent in the saddle. Everett led us across some of the most fantastic landscape in all of Wyoming. We rode along picturesque, vodka-clear creeks, through basins and glacier moraines above timberline, and along trails etched in scree rock far above the canyon bottoms.

Action came quick the next morning. After riding only a few miles, we spotted two bulls in a valley surrounded by forests. Our approach was foiled by a herd of deer that spooked and alerted the elk. The bulls were well out of range when they dashed into heavy timber.

An hour later, we witnessed an unbelievable scene. As we rode along a creek, we heard a sudden thunder of hooves in the timber. Seconds later, a herd of about 60 elk exploded from the trees and ran across the stream in front of us.

Judi and Matt were off their horses instantly, but the animals were bunched too tightly. At least five bulls, including two very good animals, were in the group. There was no chance for a shot. The risk of hitting more than one elk was too high.

The dust had hardly settled when the bull I mentioned at the beginning of this article showed up, running hard down the mountain. We didn't know whether he was part of the big band or was a loner, spooked by the rushing herd.

Now it was over, and we prepared to follow the bull that Judi had hit after the wild chase. I desperately wanted him to be lying dead close by, but I had little optimism. A nagging feeling told me we were in for a tough search.

My fears were confirmed after we followed a skimpy blood trail for a quarter mile. Judi grew more and more distraught as we went on, and I began to wonder if I was wrong about the bull being hit in a vital spot. I reassured myself that the elk was hit well, and I was determined to find the bull, no matter how long or hard the ordeal.

Judi's mood swung from despair to hope. Every time we'd find a bit of blood, I'd see a trace of a smile, but when we had difficulty

One of my proudest moments in the elk woods.

finding the next, she'd sink back into a depression.

At one point, when the sporadic trail led across a rockslide just beneath timberline, Judi walked over and held my hand.

"I really love elk hunting, Daddy," she said. "I hope I can go again with you next year."

"You will, honey," I said. "You will."

"Do you think we'll ever find my bull?" she asked.

I looked at her tear-stained face and straightened her hat. "There's no doubt in my mind," I lied. "We'll follow him to Idaho and even Montana if we have to."

At that Judi laughed, the first time I'd heard her laugh all day. Matt and Everett laughed too, and we followed the trail with renewed enthusiasm.

Three hours later I was almost convinced we'd lose the elk. There was an occasional blood spot every 10 or 20 yards; and several minutes of crawling and intent searching led us from one crimson speck to the other. Many times we lost the trail for 15 or 20 minutes until picking it up again.

The bull was heading through a jungle of thick timber down the mountain toward a steep, remote canyon. The outlook was gloomy, and I had never been so discouraged in all my years of hunting.

I was on my hands and knees, looking for clues, when Matt made the announcement that I will remember for the rest of my life.

"There he is," Matt said, "in that thicket just ahead."

Indeed, Judi's bull had come to the end of the trail. He was a dandy, with six points to the side, and he was the most welcome bull I'd seen in 25 years of hunting elk.

Judi and I walked hand in hand toward the fallen animal, and she looked at the bull a long time before speaking.

"Thanks for taking me elk hunting, Daddy," she said. "I really enjoyed it."

"I enjoyed it too, kid," I said, "but the next time you shoot an elk, make it a little easier on your old man's nervous system. I was a wreck."

"I'm the one who was supposed to be shook up, not you. You're a veteran elk hunter," she joked.

"And so are you," I responded. "After what we've been through today, so are you, sweetie."

WHEN IT'S OKAY TO KISS YOUR HORSE

Just like in the movies!

Vin Sparano and I had great aspirations of killing a couple of giant bulls in Montana. I was especially hopeful for Vin, because we'd hunted together in Idaho's Selway Wilderness and he didn't get an elk. Vin is Executive Editor of OUTDOOR LIFE, and hunts with me often in the West.

Our hunt was with outfitter Keith Rush, and Jack Atcheson Sr., a hunter's booking agent from Butte, Montana.

Atcheson and I had hunted together a number of times. I always enjoy his company because he's a great guy and a superb hunter, and it's fun listening to Jack describe hunts he'd had with Jack O'Connor, Warren Page, and many other famous gun writers.

Vin was also great company. He'd taken big caribou, mule deer, antelope, and whitetails on hunts that we'd made together, but so far our one elk hunt had been unproductive for him. I took a bull on that hunt, largely by accident, and now it was Vin's turn for an elk. (The story is recounted in another chapter in this book).

It was mid-November, and bitterly cold. A good blanket of snow on the ground betrayed elk movements.

Prior to our hunt, I'd taken Vin into Yellowstone Park to photograph some wildlife and to see Old Faithful. It was one of those rare years when Yellowstone hadn't been closed by November. Usually, enough snow falls to shut the park down until the following spring.

After viewing and photographing some deer and elk, we drove to Old Faithful and sat on the bleachers, waiting for the geyser to erupt. There wasn't a soul in sight, and it was eerie sitting there amidst plumes of steam venting out of the ground. I'd taken friends to see Old Faithful before, but there were always crowds around.

Finally, the famous geyser started up, and we watched as it boiled out of the ground and exploded into the air. It was over in seconds.

"That was it?" Vin said. "We froze our butts off for almost an hour and a half, and that was it? I thought it would erupt for several minutes."

"Were you expecting a Mt. St. Helens?" I answered. "That's it. You can tell your grandkids you saw Old Faithful in the middle of the winter when all the sane people were snug and comfortable at home."

At that we headed for my truck, broke open a thermos of hot coffee, and headed for Keith's elk camp.

The grand plan was to hunt on horseback out of base camp. We'd drive to the jump-off spot, unload the horses, and head for the snowy mountains.

The first morning was bitterly cold, down around 10 degrees below zero. I wasn't looking forward to climbing into a frozen saddle and sitting on a horse for several hours, but that's what we had to do.

Our party included Vin and I, Jack, Keith, and two guides, Mike and Kevin. Kevin is Keith's son, and is one of the finest guides I've ever known. I had just met him on that hunt, but we've since hunted together many times. There was also another hunter whose name I don't recall. He was a good friend of Keith's, and I'll call him Charley.

It didn't take long to get bone-chilling cold, despite our warm clothing. Sitting still up on a horse doesn't allow any exercise, so every now and then we'd dismount and walk a ways. When we warmed up, we'd get back on the horses and ride some more.

We were about eight miles from the trucks when a bunch of elk took off across a basin. They'd spotted us, and were moving higher up on the mountain.

Our party split up. Keith and Kevin followed the big herd of elk to see what they were up to, while the rest of us rode through the snowy timber to look for more elk. We would rendezvous at a designated area at noon and have lunch.

The country was brutal, with lots of ice, deep snow, and very steep in spots. At one point, we decided to cross a mountain afoot and have a look on the other side. Elk sign was everywhere; we expected to see animals any time.

Instead of walking around the base, Jack hiked straight up it while the rest of us walked through deep snow at the bottom. That was typical of Jack. If there's an easy way and a hard way to hunt, he'll always pick the hard way.

Later we met for lunch, and Keith announced they'd caught up with the elk. They were bedded under a rim in a draw a couple miles from our location. Keith humored us by saying that they snuck up so close to the elk they could have filled their tags with handguns. He humored us even more by saying there were three bulls in the bunch, a six-point, raghorn, and a spike.

A plan was hatched, and Keith suggested that Vin, Jack, and I take positions at vantage points along the draw. Keith, Kevin and Mike would make a big circle on horseback and try to run the elk back down the draw. Charley would take our horses and wait at the bottom of the draw. When the drivers showed up, which should be about dark, we'd go down to where Charley was, get our horses, and ride up the other side of the draw to the trucks, that is, if the elk weren't cooperative and didn't run down the draw.

Sounded easy enough, but Murphy's Law was about to make a profound impact on the simple strategy.

Vin and I took up good positions, Jack crossed the draw and waited on the other side, and Charley led the four horses down the draw, where he'd wait for us at the creek.

The elk didn't cooperate, and at dark, Vin, Jack and I headed down into the draw. The slopes were steep, rocky, and layered with snow two feet deep.

We came to the trail made by Charley and the horses, and followed it, assuming, of course, that Charley would be waiting below.

Wrong assumption. We came to the spot where Charley obviously had been waiting. In the quickly fading light that remained, we saw where he'd tied the horses, but he wasn't there. Neither were the horses.

We waited until Keith, Kevin, and Mike showed up.

"What happened to the elk?" I said to Keith.

"Sons a guns took off the wrong way," he said. "We almost had

Kevin Rush – one of Montana's finest guides, looks for elk in heavy timber.

them headed down, but they weren't having it. Where's Charley and the horses?"

"Don't know," I said. "Here's the spot where he was waiting, but he's gone."

There was enough starlight and reflection off the snow to see a bit. Keith, Kevin and Mike rode around the area, trying to figure out where Charley had gone.

Soon I heard some cussing. Keith rode up, and he wasn't happy

"Charley headed down the crick," Keith announced. "He'll never make it. The draw narrows down, and there are waterfalls ten feet deep in the bottom. The timber is too thick to get horses through and there are blowdown everywhere. He's gonna get himself in a jam."

Keith suggested we wait awhile. There were elk trails everywhere, and it would take some time to sort them out and follow Charley. The deep powder snow made it tough to differentiate between horse, man, and elk tracks. There were also moose in the area, which made tracking even more complicated.

Nope–These aren't moonshiners looking for the law – they're Montana guides and hunters.

We waited 45 minutes, and Keith returned. They still hadn't found Charley, and now it was fairly dark. Keith told us to climb back out of the basin, hit the main trail, and hike down it, while he continued looking for our horses. Kevin and Mike were in the thick forest, also looking for Charley. If they found the horses, they'd bring them to us on the trail.

It was a good plan, but Murphy was still lurking.

Jack, Vin, and I hiked slowly out of the basin in the dark. It was rough going, and it took us more than an hour to find the trail.

I should explain at this point that there were trails everywhere. A bunch of elk can make a good trail when they walk single file through the forest, and it was impossible to tell what kind of critters made the tracks in the snow. That might sound like we were lousy woodsmen, but that's nonetheless how it was. Powder snow is the worst possible medium to track something in.

We got on a major trail, and followed it for about an hour and a half. Starlight filtered down through the foliage just enough for us to see, and it was slow going.

Suddenly Keith rode up, and his voice sounded cheery.

"We ain't found Charley, yet," Keith said. "He's all messed up in that crick bottom."

"That's okay," I said, "we're having great fun strolling around in the woods. Real romantic, especially when we climb these fun slopes."

"Mebbe that explains why you're headed the way you are," Keith said. "You boys are headed for Idyho. Camp is in Montana."

"You're kidding," Jack said.

"Ain't kidding," Keith said.

At that, Jack turned on his flashlight and fished out his compass. I walked to a little clearing and looked up at the Big Dipper.

"Damn," I said, when I'd located the North Star. "We're headed for Idyho."

"Sure are," Jack said. "We're damned sure headed for Idyho."

To make matters worse, we weren't on the right trail. Finally we sorted it all out, and continued our hike, this time headed for Montana. Idyho was behind us, where it was supposed to be all along.

After another two hours, we broke out of the heavy timber and entered an area that was fairly open with patches of trees. Now that we were in the open, we could see fairly well in the starlight.

At one point, we spotted three moose beds in the snow. We'd recognized the depressions, having seen them during the day. For the first time, I was certain that we were indeed on the right trail.

Keith rode up again, announced that Charley hadn't yet been found, and quickly rode off. I think he was starting to worry about Charley. Keith never gets very upset about much of anything, but this time he was a bit concerned.

We took one of our several breaks, and discussed Charley's plight, wondering why in the world he ever left the meeting spot in the first place. Of course, we all hoped for Charley's safety, but we nevertheless had a few choice words to say about his disappearance, especially when we were slogging through deep snow, and making very little time.

Every now and then we'd hit a stream. Jack would break through the ice and scoop water out in a tin cup he'd brought along in his pack. The water was sweet and icy, and even though the temperature was around 15 below zero, as we learned later, we sweated profusely. We didn't sit still very long in one place. Exercise was necessary to keep warm. Without it, we'd be in bad trouble.

Several times we considered building a fire, but we always discounted the idea and kept going. We knew we were on the right trail, and even if we didn't get the horses back, we could walk the 10 miles to the truck in five or six hours. Sooner or later the trail would head down the mountain and we'd make better time.

About an hour later, Vin spotted a glow far ahead of us. We walked another hundred yards, and saw that it was a fire. Maybe, just maybe, Murphy would go home and we'd be out of this mess.

We walked faster, encouraged by the fire, and Keith appeared on the trail.

"We found Charley and the horses," he said, "and we got a big fire goin'. Want me to bring the horses up the trail?"

"Nah," Jack answered. "We're really into this hiking. We'll meet you at the fire."

"Where'd you find Charley?" I asked.

"He was wallerin' around in that nightmare jungle in the crick bottom," Keith said. "Good thing Kevin found him, or Charley might not have made it out of there."

When we reached the fire, Vin headed straight for his horse.

"Watch this, Zumbo," Vin said.

He walked up to his horse and planted a kiss on the horse's head.

"Why don't you kiss the other end," Jack suggested.

We had a good laugh, ate a bunch of cookies that were in the saddlebags, and warmed up around the fire.

No one said anything to Charley. He was probably badly embarrassed – no use making him feel any worse. We were glad he wasn't hurt.

We learned that Mike's horse had played out, and couldn't make it out of the bottom. Mike unsaddled and unbridled the horse and turned him free. Sooner or later, after he'd rested, the horse would walk back to camp.

It was still about eight miles to the trucks. I walked most of the way, as it was downhill, and the trail was good at that point. Now and then I'd get on the horse, and Murphy struck one last time, for both Vin and I.

While riding in the dark, a branch struck Vin's eye and scratched the cornea. At about the same time, when I was riding, my horse slipped on the icy trail. I quickly jumped out of the stirrups, hit the side of the trail, and the horse rolled over my legs. My ankle was sprained badly, but not so badly that I couldn't hobble out the rest of the way.

It was a great set of circumstances. Vin was blind, and I was crippled. The first day of our elk hunt was probably our last for the season.

We didn't give up, however. Vin put a patch over his eye, and I managed to sit on a horse, though I couldn't bend my injured leg enough to get my boot in the stirrups. I rode with one foot in the

Jack Atcheson during a happier moment. It would be a long night before it was over.

stirrups, the other dangling over the side.

The rest of the hunt was uneventful for elk. We saw more animals, but I couldn't move quickly enough when I had to, and Vin was in pain and couldn't see them very well. It's tough to see out of one eye when you aren't used to it.

I did, however, manage to collect a five-point muley buck. Kevin and I were riding off the mountain one evening when we spotted the buck and a dozen does. They didn't see us, and the buck was pretty busy romancing the does. The deer rut was in full swing.

Kevin held my horse while I hobbled along with the help of a walking stick. I walked about 500 yards, keeping a knoll between me and the deer. Then I crawled up to the top, peeked over, and saw the deer about 90 yards away. The buck was consorting with a doe, and I'm sure he went down with a smile on his face when my bullet took him.

As I always say, a little pain and suffering are often a requirement in elk hunting. Just ask me or Vin. We can tell you all about it.

A GENERAL NAMED YEAGER

Will that be one worm or two...Sir?!

I was barely out of kindergarten when a U.S. Air Force pilot became the first man in history to break the speed of sound. Most Americans are aware that Chuck Yeager was that pilot, and many came to know him through the Academy Award-winning movie, THE RIGHT STUFF, and through his books, YEAGER and PRESS ON.

Growing up next to Stewart Air Force Base in New York State, I watched and listened to jets every day. I'd hope to be a jet pilot, but I had to start wearing glasses when I was 14, so my hopes were dashed.

The opportunity to meet Chuck Yeager came in 1986. My friend, Mike Cusack, owns King Salmon Lodge in King Salmon, Alaska, and I'd fished out of the lodge several times.

Mike is a physician in Anchorage, and started out building a modest dwelling for his family. His plans changed, and instead he constructed a lovely lodge that was intended to outrageously pamper his guests.

The food is cooked by master chefs, and nothing is compromised when it comes to quality, be it food or drink. Three bush planes and a dozen boats outside the lodge are available to cater to fishermen.

Each day, anglers decide what they want to fish for, and the pilots divide the guests into parties and fly out to various lakes and streams. Those who elect to stay at the lodge can fish for giant king salmon within a few hundred yards of the front door.

Some of Mike's guests included Bob Hope, Dorothy Hamil, Ted Williams, and many other celebrities. Chuck Yeager was to be a guest in 1986, and Mike asked if I'd like to fish the same week that Yeager would be at the lodge.

My answer was an enthusiastic yes. I'd heard much about Yeager's outdoor talents, as well as his flying skills, of course, and I was overwhelmed at the chance to meet him in person.

I'll admit I was nervous when I arrived at Mike's lodge. I don't know why — perhaps the idea of meeting one of America's heroes was a heady thought.

Yeager showed up a couple hours after I did. He was with his son, Don, and there were about 20 other guests in the lodge.

When I was introduced to Yeager, he shook hands and grinned. "I know your work," he said. "I read OUTDOOR LIFE."

You could have knocked me over with a feather. The thought of Yeager reading my stuff and recognizing my name was beyond comprehension.

From that point on, Chuck Yeager became a real person. I got to know him well, as he and Don and I fished as a team throughout the week.

He was everything I'd heard him to be. A superb outdoorsman, and an interesting guy to be around.

One of the greatest moments of my life occurred when Yeager piloted our bush plane one day. I can't describe my feelings when he strapped himself into the pilot's seat and flew the Beaver float plane.

Before he flew, Mike's lodge manager called the insurance company to ask about any restrictions that might prevent Yeager from flying. The conversation went something like this:

"We'd like permission for one of our guests to fly one of the bush planes."

"No way."

"But this person is special."

"No way."

"His name is Chuck Yeager."

"I don't care who he........GENERAL Chuck Yeager....you mean

Chuck Yeager looks at elk country. He is an expert horseman and hunter.

THE RIGHT STUFF......speed of sound.......the best pilot in the world?"

"Yeah."

"He can fly any damned plane he wants."

"Thanks."

Chuck piloted the airplane with incredible ease, flying low and fast over the tundra. His takeoffs and landings were flawless, and his incredible eyesight allowed him to spot caribou, moose, and brown bears long before anyone else in the airplane.

Since that first trip, I've been fortunate to have fished and hunted with Chuck Yeager a number of times. Of all those outings, our elk hunts were special. Two of them are recounted elsewhere in this book.

Yeager is depicted as a crusty, stern General. That might be the way he comes across in the military, but when he's outdoors he's eloquent and almost poetic. Deep in his eyes you can see his love of wild things and wild places. The man was raised in the outback of West Virginia, and grew up with a fishing rod and a gun in his hands. He's never lost his touch. If anything, he's even closer to the outdoors than ever before.

On our first elk hunt, I watched him closely as he rode a horse. His knowledge of horses and horsemanship was obvious. He was in total command, riding with ease and confidence.

Chuck Yeager isn't much for camp discipline. He'd much rather hunt on his own, but when the hunt requires a guide, Yeager quickly rearranges the strategy.

Here's how a typical dialog will go:

"What's the plan for today," Yeager says to his guide.

"We'll hunt in the morning, come in for lunch, and later go out for an afternoon hunt," the guide responds.

"Why do we have to come in for lunch?"

"Well, we just do it to take a break in midday, General."

"How 'bout we skip comin' into camp, and hunt all day? To hell with the break."

"Whatever you want, General. We can do that if you'd like."

"Now then, see that big 'ol mountain up there in the clouds? I bet there's a hell of a bull on it. Let's go take a look."

"Okay, General. Let's go look."

And that's the way it goes with Chuck. He's the first one up in the morning, the first one out of camp, and the last one in at night.

One guide remarked to me one evening: "That man is as tough as a boot. He's 40 years older than me, and I had to go like hell to stay in front of him. I can't believe it."

While hunting in Colorado, Chuck and I headed down into a basin while Frank Simms, our outfitter, hiked up onto a high ridge to glass for elk.

Yeager easily bounced along on the treacherous rocks left by glaciers, and he seemed as happy as I'd ever seen him. He'd already taken his bull, and I was still looking for mine. We settled into a comfortable spot and sat there until nightfall.

While we waited, Yeager talked freely about the wonders of the mountains. He was obviously very much at home, and he shared some feelings about hunting and the outdoors. I was touched that he'd discuss those ideals with me.

Yeager is often impatient with minor civilized rules, and bends the law accordingly. Once, when we were driving to a hunt, we stopped in a town to buy some gear. It was rush hour, traffic was heavy. Each of us was driving a vehicle.

When we came back out of a store, Yeager looked up and down the street, noting the traffic.

"I'm gonna just nose out and make a U-turn," he said. "It'll take too much time to go around the block."

Yeager and I pose with his Colorado elk. It was his biggest elk ever.

"You're going to try a U-turn in that traffic?" I asked.

"Sure. Just follow me," he said.

Yeager did, and I followed. General Chuck Yeager was making an illegal maneuver on the street, and seemed pleased to do so. He wasn't a bit phased.

Another time Chuck and I were returning from a salmon fishing trip on the Oregon coast. He was riding in a vehicle with one of the anglers in our party, and I followed. The angler was about to turn off the Interstate on an exit where Chuck was supposed to get out and ride with me the rest of the way.

Rather than make the turn off the ramp, Yeager told the driver to stop along the Interstate where he'd get out. It didn't matter that stopping along a busy Interstate was only for emergencies. We unloaded the General's gear and transferred it to my truck.

"It's a damned lot easier to make the switch here rather than go all the way out the exit ramp," he said. I agreed, of course, amazed at the man's spunk and attitude.

Yeager is constantly hounded by autograph seekers, no matter where he is. I've been with him in airports, restaurants, hotel lobbies, sport expos, or just walking down the street. He is recognized everywhere, and I've never known him to balk at signing his autograph.

A few years ago, I asked Chuck if he'd be Grand Marshal for the Fourth of July festivities in Cody, Wyoming, where I live. A number of celebrities, including John Wayne, have served as Grand Marshal in the past. At first Chuck declined, but then he asked if there were any golden trout in Wyoming.

"Lots of goldens in the Wind River Range," I said.

"Real high country?" he asked.

"Real high. Absolutely beautiful."

"If you'll backpack with me, I'll be Grand Marshal, but we fish for 10 days."

"It's a deal."

As it turned out, Chuck's wife, Glennis, needed some medical attention. He cancelled the fishing trip, but lived up to his promise to be Grand Marshal.

Before he came, he laid down some rules.

"I don't want to go to any fancy cocktail parties or luncheons," he said. "Let's do some fishin', and you can show me the country in that beat up truck of yours."

We fished, and shot hand-thrown clay targets in my back yard. I barbecued some elkburgers, and introduced him to friends. The high rollers in town were dying to have him at their houses for parties, but Yeager would have none of it. He was content to just maintain a low profile and relax.

When he was Grand Marshal for the parade, he rode down the street in a convertible. Dozens of youngsters ran after him, wanting him to sign autographs. The parade came to a halt frequently while Yeager gave autographs to the mobs of kids. He insisted on signing every request. It was a slow parade.

It was satisfying to later watch Chuck Yeager and Bob Hope serve as Grand Marshals for President Bush's Inaugural Parade in 1988. As I watched on TV, I remembered him in the little town of Cody, and when I saw that famous grin, I was betting he'd rather be fishing or hunting rather than surrounded by thousands of people.

He's one of a kind, and I fully understand why he has the right stuff. I'm convinced he'll never say to heck with elk hunting, no matter what.

I SWEAR I AIMED BETWEEN HIS EYES, SEÑOR

If you've studied elk biology much, you're probably aware that their international name is wapiti. Taxonomists (those people who classify critters into genuses and species) say that our American elk and the European red deer are the same. Technically, our elk and the red deer are classified by the same exact genus and species – Cervus elaphus.

Now then, I've hunted the red deer, also called the red stag, and looked at several real close. Close, meaning dead at my feet. As far as I'm concerned, they don't look anything like our elk, and they don't vocalize like ours, either.

The stag is much smaller than our elk, is a different color, has a different horn structure, and has a thicker snout. It also doesn't make the sweet bugle as our guy. Instead, it utters an awful roar that sounds like an old Hereford cow in the pasture.

But I'm not qualified to argue with the expert scientists who study such matters, so I'll accept their opinion. As a former wildlife biologist myself, I know that a lot of study and research goes into taxonomy work.

I took my red deer on a hunt in Spain hosted by Zeiss, the German optics company that manufactures some of the very finest binoculars and rifle scopes in the world.

Also included on the hunt were nine other American gun and hunting writers. The purpose of the hunt was to use and evaluate some new Zeiss products on an actual hunt. Not a bad deal, eh?

Bruce Cavey, an official with the Zeiss corporate office in the U.S., put the trip together, and joined us on the hunt.

Our group met in New York, which was our takeoff point for Madrid. After landing and going through customs, we boarded a bus and rode to Ricardo Medem's estate, called Cazatur. On the way, we visited Toledo, a charming and historic city known for producing the finest swords in the world.

Senor Medem's hunting Lodge was a bit different than I'm used to in the Rockies. It definitely was a departure from the routine elk camp.

We would live in a castle-type lodge during the hunt. Each of us had our own bedroom and bath, and a maid cleaned the room every day. I wasn't accustomed to such pampering, and decided there and then to speak with a few outfitters I know back home in Wyoming. They should learn some class from these fancy Spaniards.

I noted that all the windows in the castle had iron bars on the outside. Back in the old days, the owner was either trying to keep some people in, or some people out. I never found out which.

Meals were outstanding. There was lots of great cheese with each meal, fine wine, and a whole bunch of cerveza (beer) which we consumed at various times during the day, with the exception of the periods prior to our hunting.

After eating lunch on the first day, the next project was to go to the shooting range where we'd be assigned rifles and ammo, followed by target practice.

The folks at Remington had generously contributed all the rifles and ammo for the hunt. Of course, they were all topped with Zeiss's finest scopes. I was issued a 7mm Mag.

At the range, the head guide made an amazing announcement.

"The average shot," he said, "will be at least 200 yards, and it

Do not ask Zumbo where he aimed.

probably will be offhand."

"Offhand?" we all said in disbelief. "Two-hundred yards?"

"The brush is very high," the guide explained. "In most situations you can't see the animal from a prone, sitting, or kneeling position."

In order to practice, we shot at a five-inch metal disk at 200 yards – offhand. Our success at hitting it will not be revealed, but it was mighty poor.

If you think we were lousy shots (our party included some of the best marksmen in the writing business), give it a try, but expect to be embarrassed if there are onlookers who watch you miss – and miss. A five-inch target is about as big as a large grapefruit, and 200 yards offhand is a long, long, ways.

Each of us was given a choice of taking a red deer, mouflon sheep, or fallow deer. Of course, I opted for the red deer.

Hunting was done from Land Rovers. Each group of hunters was assigned a guide, and we were told which animals to shoot. The strategy was simple. We'd merely ride around the brushy country of the large estate until a good animal appeared. Then we'd get out and shoot.

If this doesn't sound sporting, remember that we were in a foreign country, participating in a hunt with rules established by the landowner. When in Spain, do as the Spaniards do, as they say.

I was the last to take an animal. It happened that our entire group was loaded in two vehicles, driving along, when a nice stag appeared in a large opening.

The guide nodded to me, and I got out. Because there was no intervening brush, I was able to shoot from a kneeling position. It was getting dark, and the stag was about 250 yards out.

I was nervous. Here I was, about to make a fairly long shot, with nine of the top gun writers in the U.S. looking on.

I should point out that when you write about something, no matter what, your readers judge you to be an expert on the subject

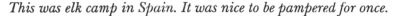

This was elk camp in Spain. It was nice to be pampered for once.

you write about. Your peers are, however, mighty curious about your REAL expertise. Some writers write good, but they aren't worth a darn when it comes time to doing what they write about.

Imagine then, my apprehension at being watched by my peers. They were no doubt thinking, "what is Zumbo REALLY like with a gun in his hands?"

As I drew a bead on the stag, he stopped walking and looked at me, as if on cue, and I fired.

It was wonderful. The animal dropped to the ground hard, and a great feeling of relief swept over me. My companions congratulated me on the shot.

When we approached the stag, we saw that my bullet had hit him squarely between the eyes, though his head was still quite intact.

"What a shot, Zumbo," someone quipped, "right between the eyes." There were more congratulations from my amazed pals.

Please don't ask if I aimed between the stag's eyes. That's a secret I'll never divulge, even in this book of confessions.

There's no way I'll ever tell. What the heck, every guy has a little pride.

Besides, I want every one of those writers to remember that shot. I need all the help I can get.

MADNESS ON THE FIRING LINE

Oldtimers who have kept up with elk hunting over the years are familiar with the famous firing line near Gardiner, Montana. The place gets its name from the small army of hunters who waited each year for elk migrating out of Yellowstone Park to cross into the hunting area on the Gallatin National Forest.

The old joke around Gardiner saloons was that you didn't need a rifle to get an elk — just a tag and a pair of tennis shoes. The first ones to the fallen bulls claimed them.

Happily, the firing line no longer exists, but when it did, chaos reigned supreme. Literally hundreds of hunters ambushed elk spewing out of Yellowstone. It was nothing for a herd of 20 to 30 bulls to be exterminated in a few seconds.

While this might sound savage, consider the alternative. Without hunting, the elk were committed to dying via "nature's way", which typically meant slow, agonizing starvation over the course of several cruel months. A bullet was a merciful solution.

My first look at the firing line was with Gabby Barrus, a photographer pal from Cody, Wyoming. Gabby and I were taking pictures of elk in Yellowstone, and I happened to have an unpunched Montana elk license. We decided to take the short ride from Gardiner to look over the firing line area. I had no idea what to expect, and was most curious.

We drove up the road toward Jardine, which is a tiny gold-mining town near Gardiner, and saw enough to immediately discourage me from unlimbering my rifle. Hunters were in every conceivable location. I counted 116 from where I stood. A pair of hunters had built a snow blind that resembled a roughly built igloo; other hunters were positioned every place that an elk might pass.

We watched a bunch of elk trot down through the ranks of people, and every animal met its destiny on the slopes. From then on it was mayhem as hunters ran about tagging their elk.

As the years passed, the Montana Department of Fish, Wildlife, and Parks, trimmed the hunt area to the point where the firing line no longer existed. Popular areas were placed off-limits, requiring hunters to change their strategies.

One year, I visited the Gardiner hunting area with Hal Mecham, an outfitter buddy from Utah. Hal was just getting into wildlife photography, and I'd taken him into Yellowstone to photograph elk, deer, and sheep.

We'd gone up into the famous elk hunting area with Don Laubach and his son, Kirk, who had an elk tag. Don lives in Gardiner, and is a superb elk hunter in his own right.

Our vantage point was from a ridge overlooking a slope on the opposite side of a stream below us. We drank coffee and chatted in the dark, waiting for shooting light.

When it was light enough to shoot, Don spotted something far below us. We looked to see a bull elk in an opening. Several hunters saw the elk too, but Kirk collected it nicely.

We ran down the steep slope, crossed the creek on an icy, slippery log, and hiked up the opposite mountainside to the elk. While Don and Kirk were dressing it, a barrage of shots broke out over the ridge. I'd seen some deer trot across the ridge when we were headed for the elk, and assumed that hunters were shooting at the deer, which were also legal game besides elk.

Later I learned that a herd of 14 bulls had been ambushed by a large party of hunters. All the elk were taken; every one of them had a rack that was six points or better.

There are two types of rifle elk hunts in the Gardiner area. The first is the standard five week season which traditionally starts in October and ends the Sunday of Thanksgiving weekend. The other is a special late hunt which requires a lottery draw for a tag. In the case of the latter, the season runs in January and February, and hunts are two or four days, depending on the type of tag drawn. The computer selects hunt dates for successful applicants.

Though I've applied for late tags, I've never drawn one. Twice I accompanied other hunters who had tags. Both hunted with outfitter Bill Hoppe, whose lovely ranch home is literally in the migration path of elk traveling out of Yellowstone.

Mary Lineback of Billings drew a tag, and she took a beautiful six-point bull after hunting only an hour. It was hard to tell who was more excited — Mary or her husband. Nonetheless, she scored on a dandy elk that most hunters would fantasize about.

The other hunter I accompanied was Spencer Kaylor, a young 12-year-old boy who earned an elk hunting degree in a hurry. The youngster collected a massive six-point bull that had been standing about 75 yards from where Mary had shot her bull three years before.

I had been involved in shooting a late-season elk hunting video with SPORTSMEN ON FILM when Spencer took his bull. The cameraman recorded it all nicely, and Spencer performed his part well. His bull put the finishing touches on the video production.

The most humorous incident in the late season area occurred when Don Laubach and I were filming hunters. Don carried a video camera, and this was back in the days when videos hadn't yet become very popular. Don's was an early model that required heavy batteries that had to be backpacked.

At one point, a hunter appeared on a slope about 300 yards away from us. At the same time, we saw two four-point bulls down in a draw between us and the hunter.

Don started filming when the hunter took aim at one of the bulls. The elk hit the ground hard at the shot, and the hunter then fired at the other bull, knocking it down two yards from the first. All the while, Don kept his camera trained on the scene, recording the incident.

The hunter hurried down to the elk, and we saw him raise his rifle and finish one of the bulls.

Suddenly another person appeared. It was a game warden, who hadn't witnessed the shooting, but had come along to check the hunter. The hunter tried to claim that someone else had killed the second bull.

The warden asked us if we'd seen the hunter shoot. Don pointed to his video and said that not only had we seen it, but it was duly recorded on film.

We climbed up to Bill Hoppe's ranch house and enjoyed a cup of coffee while the hunter and warden watched the scene unfold on the TV. There, it became perfectly clear that the man had killed both elk.

No further questions were asked, the man accepted his fine gracefully, and he no doubt said to heck with elk hunting when all was said and done.

IT HAPPENED IN THREES

Colorado has the distinction of having more elk than any other state. It also has more hunters, and they take more elk than anywhere else.

That's all fine and dandy, but there are zillions of hunters wherever there is good access on public land. National forests and BLM lands are swarming with people, giving the first-time hunter to the West a rude awakening. Unfortunately, some of the wide-open spaces have just as many hunters per square mile as many of the more populated eastern states.

One year, I hunted Colorado with two companions. My pal, Hal Mecham, his friend Jeff, and I loaded up our horses and made camp in the mountains a couple days before the opener.

We knew of a good spot that usually held elk, but other people knew about it, too. We were willing to gamble, and scouted for two full days prior to the season. There were a bunch of elk around, and we'd located several herds.

We left camp long before daylight on opening morning. Hal and Jeff rode horseback to a canyon close to camp, while I left my horse in camp and walked.

I found a good vantage point where I could see much of the canyon's slopes and watched. Daylight was typically slow in arriving, and when it did, I heard a shot in the bottom.

Moments later I heard an animal crashing through a very narrow strip of brush that ran vertically up the opposing slope from where I sat. Try as I might, I couldn't see the animal, though occasionally I saw brush move as it went through.

The sounds continued for almost a full minute. It was frustrating to sit there and not make out the source of the noise.

After waiting awhile, I eased down the mountain and found Hal and Jeff dressing out a five-point bull. Jeff had ridden up on the animal just at shooting light and had quickly gotten a bullet into it.

The noise I'd heard was made by a six-point bull making his escape up through the strip of brush. Jeff had spotted it after he shot the five-pointer, and Hal wasn't there to shoot the bigger bull.

I was amazed that the bull stayed in that slice of cover all the way to the top and over. That critter was thinking like a whitetail deer.

The next morning, we headed for another area. There were plenty of hunters in the canyon; no elk in his right mind would go back in there for a long time. Jeff was fortunate that he'd seen the bull first. I counted two dozen hunters in there, and those were just the ones I saw.

Our second day's efforts would involve a sashay through some timber where we'd seen elk before the opener. Jeff rode along for the heck of it with Hal, and I tied my horse and walked down a lovely grassy valley hemmed in by a thick fir forest on one side and quaking aspens on the other. The little valley was barely 50 yards wide at its widest spot.

Not a bad double, when you consider the woods were crawling with hunters around us.

I eased along, sort of lost in the beauty of the place. The aspens were a riot of color—gold, yellow, and orange. They are to the Rocky Mountains what the sugar maples are to New England, and I never tire of looking at autumn foliage.

An old trapper's cabin at the very bottom of the glade caught my attention. I walked over and investigated it, and pictured the lifestyle of the former occupants. The cabin was in bad shape, with a rotted roof, and badly deteriorating walls. The windows and door were missing, and packrats had taken it over.

I ate a sandwich at the cabin, still conjuring images in my brain of what the cabin's owner saw when he awoke every morning. It was one of the most magnificent places I'd ever seen, completely secluded, yet alive with all the outdoors.

Reluctantly I headed back up the little valley, intending to walk to the top and begin stillhunting the thick timber.

It took me a half hour to hike up, and when I did, I had the urge to carve my initials in a dead aspen tree next to the glade. I sat down on the forest floor and carved. It took me about 20 minutes, and when I was done, I began walking away.

Suddenly I heard a branch pop in the timber. It was loud enough to have been made by a large animal or a person. I discounted a squirrel or small mammal.

I ran across to the opposite side, quickly settled down in some brush, and heard another branch pop. Presently a cow elk ran across the opening below me.

I raised my rifle, and three more elk ran out of the timber — two cows and a five-point bull. I quickly centered the bull, squeezed the trigger, and he folded at the edge of the opening.

Absolutely amazing. If I hadn't had the strange compulsion to carve my initials in the tree, I'd have been out of the valley when the elk ran out.

Maybe it was ESP, maybe a hunch. Whatever, I'd been mighty lucky to have been in the right spot at the right time.

To put the frosting on the cake, Hal took a five-point bull the next day. We'd badly beaten Colorado's odds, where hunter success is normally 20 percent or less. Three bulls for three hunters was a pretty good score. I'll take that kind of luck every time I can in the elk woods.

FOUR BIG ONES IN COLORADO

Remember I told ya not t' bet against Yeager's shooting ability.

It was one of those moments that would never be forgotten, never dulled with time. The sun cast its last rays on the peaks around us, lighting them with the magic of alpenglow, a fleeting sensation of colors seen only during the first and last minutes of sunrise and sunset.

We sat quietly in a glacial basin, where stunted trees and scrub brush attested to the sterility of the scoured soil and savage weather. Our vantage point was at the edge of timberline, an inhospitable place visited by few humans, most of them infrequent elk hunters.

Chuck Yeager sat beside me, looking intently into the cirque below us. He'd seen a good bull walk into the dense spruce forest bordering the basin the previous evening, and we were hoping the elk would show.

Frank Simms, our outfitter, had climbed high on the peaks to glass the lower forested areas, leaving us to watch for the elk. If Frank saw anything decent, we'd plan a morning strategy provided the bull Yeager saw didn't cooperate.

Darkness slowly blanketed the landscape, leaving us no choice but to reluctantly leave the pristine surroundings. Chuck and I cautiously made our way across the boulder-strewn glacial moraine, using starlight to guide our way.

It was the third day of our Colorado hunt sponsored by the Rocky Mountain Elk Foundation. The hunt turned out to be everything I thought it to be, and then some. Chuck Yeager had already taken his bull, as did Cy Pellow.

Vivi Crandall and I hadn't scored yet, and I had high hopes for morning. Frank had spotted a fine bull from his lofty vantage point, and figured it might return in the morning. George Taulman, Vivi's guide, also had a good area in mind for her morning hunt.

As elk hunts go, this one couldn't honestly be considered physically tough, unless you wanted it to be. It truly was a dream hunt, with plenty of big bulls, and a large property that was exclusively ours to roam.

The four of us had opted to work hard, and we had plenty of opportunity to do so. The area we hunted was a 17,000 acre ranch composed of towering peaks and thick forests. Some of those peaks reached well above 10,000 feet into brilliantly clear, crisp skies.

The ranch's owner, Bobby Hill, was a cooperator in Colorado's Ranching For Wildlife program. By doing so, he and his clients were allowed to hunt the property with firearms during the month of September provided Hill made some tags available to the public. Those tags were issued by the Colorado Division of Wildlife in a lottery draw.

Frank and George own U.S. Outfitters, which conducts hunts on a number of Colorado and New Mexico ranches. As I soon learned, the pair were great fun to hunt elk with, and they offered some of the best elk hunts in the country, including hunts on Hill's ranch.

The hunt was born when Bob Munson, RMEF's Executive Director, and I put together a membership drive/fund raising package. The biggest hitch was to convince Chuck Yeager to go along with the project. As I figured, however, Chuck readily agreed to cooperate. His calendar was clear during the hunt dates, and to say that he loves to hunt elk would be an understatement. I've accompanied Yeager on a half-dozen hunting and fishing trips, and I knew he'd have a tough time turning the trip down.

The fund-raising part of the hunt involved auctioning off one of

Vivi Crandall has plenty of reason to smile.

the four spots at the 1989 RMEF Convention in Seattle. Vivi Crandall, a well-known artist from Wyoming, was highest bidder. Though she had taken nine elk in her life, she was looking for a trophy bull.

The membership drive aspect provided a hunt to the person who sold the most RMEF memberships during a prescribed period. Cy Pellow of Sacramento, California, earned the hunt by signing up some 300 members. Overall, the hunt was responsible for well more than 1500 new RMEF members.

The hunt was held during the last few days of September and early October, just right for bugling. The four of us had great expectations when we settled into the comfortable cabin at Hill's ranch.

Chuck Yeager needs no introduction to most Americans. In 1947, he became the first man to break the speed of sound. Most of the Academy Award winning movie, "THE RIGHT STUFF", was written around Yeager's pilot years, and, at age 67, he continues as a test pilot as I write this.

When we arrived at the cabin, Frank Simms suggested we sight in our rifles that afternoon. We drove a short distance away, set up a target, and fine-tuned our rifles.

Chuck was shooting a 7mm Magnum, and I made a small wager with him as to his ability to place a bullet three inches high on a paper plate at 100 yards. I'd hunted with Chuck before and knew his shooting skills, but I always liked to give him a hard time.

Yeager drilled the plate exactly three inches high, and then I proposed he hit the nail that fastened the paper plate to a stump. There was some good-natured kidding from Vivi, Cy, and other on-lookers, and I was truly amazed when his bullet drove the nail into the tree. So much for kidding Yeager about his shooting ability.

Frank and George suggested we try an evening hunt after we sighted our rifles. The plan was to watch some openings where elk were apt to feed in prior to dark.

We split up, and I opted to tag along with Vivi and her husband, Gary, as an observer. George would be Vivi's guide.

The meadow we watched was like a giant amoeba in a dense evergreen forest. George wanted to try a spot where he'd seen a good bull the week before. The area hadn't been hunted since, and he figured the elk might be using the meadow again.

We were slipping along the edge of the timber when we heard a bull bugle in the forest ahead of our location. After stopping to listen, we heard another bull behind us. George suggested that Vivi and I ease up where we could see the meadow's edge while he walked back to get a look at the bull behind us. Gary would stay a few steps behind Vivi and me, using a spotting scope.

Once situated, Vivi and I saw two cows enter the meadow, but a small island of trees prevented us from seeing all of the opening. Gary signaled us, gesturing that he could see the bull. Gary crawled up and suggested Vivi look it over carefully, but he didn't think it was something Vivi would be interested in so early in the hunt.

We slipped up to where we could have a better vantage point of the meadow, and we spotted the bull in a wallow, pawing mud. He was a fine animal, but Vivi decided to hold off. Our hunt was only an hour old; perhaps we could do better.

Cy and Chuck had similar stories to tell that night. Both had passed up bulls.

Cy Pellow and his huge bull. I lost the flip of a coin. The elk won Bull Of The Woods in the RMEF contest.

The next morning, Vivi, Gary, and I went back to the meadow with George. We saw some small bulls, but nothing good. As the sun rose higher, we headed into the forest, stillhunting slowly. Some of the timber was open enough where you could see a hundred yards or more. We saw only a spike bull.

Yeager took the first elk of the hunt that day, a dandy six-point with heavy beams. He and his guide, Jerry Vandiver, had hiked all day, through thick forests and across steep mountains and high ridges. In the afternoon, they heard two bulls bugling, and worked their way in close. Jerry took a position behind Chuck and blew on his cow call.

A bull charged straight in without hesitation, and, as Yeager said later, "that elk's antlers looked eight feet tall when he came tearing through the trees."

Chuck needed no time to make a decision on the bull. He drew a quick bead and made a clean kill on the animal.

A heck of a way to make a living. Frank Simms packs out Chuck Yeager's bull.

When we first heard about Yeager's bull, he told us he'd killed a two-point. Then he grinned his famous grin, and said, "with four extry points on each side." I should have known!

That evening, several of us hiked in to the bull and quartered it. Using backpacks, we hauled it out to a road about a mile away. Fortunately, most of the route was along a timbered creek, with no steep climbs.

Frank Simms and Mike Powell, who is the ranch manager, accompanied Cy and I to a different area the next morning. We hiked up a steep mountainside, intending to look for feeding bulls above timberline and in small basins.

It was a quiet morning, punctuated by the occasional bugle of an elk in the distance. We saw a mature bull with several cows about a mile away on the other side of the mountain, but he'd no doubt be in the timber before we got to him. We kept climbing.

We heard an elk bugle somewhere above us as we hiked, but we couldn't pinpoint the location of the sound. A few minutes later I looked above us and saw a herd of elk feeding in the open about 450 yards away. They were just under a very high ridge and hadn't spotted us.

Taking cover next to some trees, we decided on a strategy. Frank figured we could sneak closer to get a better look, but first we needed to generally size up the bull from where we were.

"Two bulls," Frank said after he raised his binoculars, "and both are excellent. One is just a bit better than the other. He has a wider rack, and his royal points are slightly longer."

The rest of us looked, and I was immediately impressed with both bulls. They were superb animals. The biggest bull was in the midst of the cows, while the other was just off from the herd about 50 yards away.

Cy and I flipped a coin for the biggest bull. He won, and we decided to get as close as possible before taking a shooting position. It appeared the elk were feeding in our direction.

We narrowed the distance to about 300 yards, and I checked both bulls again. This time the so-called smaller bull was standing, with the rising sun behind him backlighting his antlers. It was a gorgeous sight, and I changed my mind about the bull's size. He appeared to be just as good as the other.

We immediately discovered a monumental problem. The quickly rising sun was directly behind the elk, who were above us. It was impossible to see through our scopes.

Cy took a position, and I settled down 10 yards away. Frank held his big Stetson so it shaded Cy's scope, and when the hat was just right, Cy fired.

I tried in vain to see the other bull through the glare in my scope, and when Frank rushed over with his hat, it was too late. The bull ran into the middle of the cows, and stayed there while they ran over the ridge.

Cy's bull was impressive, with six heavy points on each side. After dressing the animal, the rest of the group showed up and helped us skid him down the mountain to a road. Vivi had no luck that morning, seeing only a few small bulls.

Late that afternoon, Chuck Yeager and I sat high along a basin near timberline that I described at the beginning of this article. When we met Frank at the truck, he said he'd seen a good bull far below. He figured the animal was worth a try in the morning.

We did just that the next day, but the bull eluded us. Frank and Mike had selected a spot to watch, but the bull evidently left before it was light enough to see. A small bull lingered in the meadow, but that was it.

We had just about decided that the bull wouldn't show when we heard a shot from Vivi's direction. She and George and Gary were about a half mile away.

Wasting no time getting there, we spotted them along the edge of a clearing. Vivi was wearing a big smile as we approached. We understood why when we looked at the lovely six-point bull lying next to the timber's edge. Vivi had taken the animal at a measured distance of 410 yards.

I wasn't surprised at the accomplishment. Vivi is an enthusiastic, knowledgeable hunter. Many men would do well to keep up with her or match her shooting abilities.

We helped get Vivi's elk back to the cabin, and Frank, Mike, and I spent the rest of the afternoon stillhunting. We saw no elk, though we didn't enter pockets of thick timber where they might be bedded. The idea was to try not to disturb animals, allowing them to come to clearings late in the afternoon.

Just before dark, Frank, Mike and I sat in the timber watching the same meadow that we observed that morning. We were tucked into a dense stand of trees, and the wind was perfect. I had a solid rest for my rifle, and when I laid the firearm on the rest and checked it out, I looked at Frank and grinned. "Meat on the table," I said.

I had a strange feeling that now it was my turn, and of all the elk hunts I'd ever been on, this was as close to perfect as possible. All my companions had taken good bulls, and I was situated in a vantage point that offered a grand finale to the hunt. If a respectable bull showed, he'd be only 200 yards out.

It was about 15 minutes before dark when the cow and calf stepped out into the meadow. The bull followed, and I knew instantly he was special. When Frank whispered for me to take him, I'd already made that decision and had my rifle resting solidly on the branch in front of me.

I waited for the elk to present just the right position, and my bullet took him in a vital area. Frank beat me over to him, and when he yelled, "seven points on each side," I was amazed. I hadn't seen the seventh points as I drew a bead on the bull.

It had indeed turned into a dream hunt for all of us. To be sure, it wasn't representative of elk hunting in the West, by any means, but

I was pleased with this one. It rounded out our foursome.

that's why it was a dream. There aren't many places where you can experience a more quality hunt. I'm still pinching myself, wondering if the whole thing really happened.

Later, Cy's bull won RMEF's Bull Of The Woods Contest. Absolutely amazing. Twice I accompanied contest winners on RMEF membership drive hunts, and twice my companions killed the Bull Of The Woods.

They say things happen in threes, and who knows. They also say the third time is the charm. Maybe the next time it'll be MY turn at Bull Of The Woods. As another old saying goes — good things come to those who wait — and wait — and wait.....and.....

IT DOESN'T GET ANY EASIER THAN THIS

Well...guess it's time t' go kill a bull.

Every now and then, every one of us that hunts elk hard should have an opportunity to do an easy hunt. I figure that's a payback for all the miserable hours spent hiking, falling, climbing outrageously steep mountains, bleeding after working through blowdowns and nightmare timber tangles, freezing, sweating, and coming into camp so bone weary that a sleeping bag is the only luxury our brains can comprehend.

I had one of those precious opportunities when the high rollers from Winchester Ammo invited me to go on their annual Sweepstakes hunt with the winner of their contest.

It was an all-expenses paid hunt on a sprawling ranch north of Bozeman, Montana. Outfitter Mike Parsons had leased the ranch, and we had exclusive hunting rights on it.

I agreed to go, without needing my arm twisted, and headed my pickup north from my home in Wyoming the day before the season opened. At the ranch I met Mike Jordan, one of Winchester's execs,

This was the site of the ambush. Two shots, two bulls – just like that

and John Pries, a nice young man from San Diego, who won the hunt out of a total of 85,000 contestants.

Accommodations were excellent. We stayed in a comfortable house on the ranch, and ate in a building next door. A Montana gal named Marie came up with some of the finest meals I've ever had, and her crazy sense of humor kept us in stitches.

All in all, there were seven hunters in the group. Besides Mike, John, and I, the other four were from Maryland. They were a bunch of husky guys, and were fun to be around. There was lots of camp humor — just the way it should be on an elk hunt.

After dinner the first night, Mike Parsons explained the strategy. Before shooting light on opening morning, Mike Jordan, John and I would head down the road in Mike Parson's pickup. We'd park the truck next to a creek, and hike across a meadow for about a half mile. If luck was on our side, there'd be a bunch of elk in a wide draw below the meadow. Mike had been watching the herd for a few days, and was fairly confident they'd be there on opening morning.

The wind gusted mightily all night long, and it was still ripping

John Pries with his "tough" Montana elk.

when we headed for the hunting area. I hoped that we wouldn't need to take any long shots if the elk were still there, because the wind drift would play nasty games with our bullets.

Mike Parsons parked the truck according to plan, and we hiked across the windy meadow. As we reached the rocky edge of the meadow above the draw, Parsons crawled up to the top and looked over. A thumbs up sign told us what we wanted to know.

"Big herd of elk below us," Mike whispered when he crawled back. "At least 80. There's a good bull in the bunch, and several smaller bulls, but it's still too dark to get a good look. There might be other big bulls that I can't see."

We'd already decided that John Pries would have his pick. Mike Jordan would shoot next, and I'd take last shot.

I doubted if I'd shoot at all. My Wyoming home is so close to Montana that it was easy for me to hunt there. I already had plans to hunt on my own elsewhere in Montana during the last week of the season if I didn't kill a bull on this hunt.

We waited for shooting light before sneaking up to the rim. When we did, I saw a nice six point bull less than 100 yards away. Several other smaller bulls were in the big herd.

The wind was still very strong, but it was blowing from the elk to us. They wouldn't pick up our scent, and the range was so short that we weren't worried about wind drift.

John and Mike Jordan found comfortable positions while Mike Parsons and I watched.

It was all over in seconds. John toppled the six-point bull neatly, and Mike Jordan's bullet scored on a four point bull.

Neither hunter had ever taken an elk before, and they were as excited as expected.

And that was that. Two tags filled two minutes after shooting light arrived.

"Hey, Zumbo," John quipped. "I thought you said this was going to be an easy hunt. Shucks, we had to walk a whole half mile from the truck, and wait 10 minutes before we could shoot. That's a lot to ask."

"I'm glad you're grinning, good buddy," I said. I could have said a whole lot more, but I broke out laughing, slapped John on the back, and called him a nasty name.

Then we ran down the hill to the elk, whooping and carrying on like a bunch of kids.

PLEASE, NO MORE BIKINIS IN ELK CAMP

What 'cha Playin?!

Being a naturally inquisitive person, especially when it comes to elk hunting, I couldn't resist investigating a very early hunt in Idaho. Amazingly enough, a gun hunt was scheduled to open August 15th, 1990. I'd heard of archery seasons opening in mid-to late August, but a firearms hunt that early was unheard of.

I called my good buddy Leon Parson, a well-known wildlife artist who lives in Rexburg. The hunt unit was in the desert and lowlands adjacent to Rexburg, so I figured Leon would have a few answers.

As it turned out, he'd never hunted the unit, preferring instead to hunt the higher mountains later in the fall, as did most all the other folks in those parts. Leon suggested I call a friend of his who knew the unit, which I did, and which he did.

The man said he'd killed a bull in the unit the year before, and he'd be willing to give me information if I drew a tag. He was not terribly enthusiastic, however. It seemed that the hunt was held early in order to exterminate a small herd of resident elk that were stealing grub from some irrigated alfalfa fields. Rather than hassling with the elk damage, the game department boys decided to get rid of the problem once and for all.

I wasn't doing much in mid-August, except working for a living by writing stories and sneaking in a little fishing now and then, so I decided to apply for the hunt. I convinced a good pal of mine, Nick Seifert, to apply with me. Nick is a young associate editor for OUTDOOR LIFE, and, being a Colorado native, was missing the Rockies. New York City isn't exactly the ideal place to headquarter an outdoor magazine, and Nick, like most of the other editors, was yearning to see mountains and blue skies.

We applied together prior to the early June deadline, and it took the bureaucracy in Boise most of the summer to figure out who had drawn tags for the special so-called "controlled" hunts around the state. They finally got their act together and told us, on August 8th, that we'd drawn tags. We had one week to plan a hunt.

Nick left New York on August 11th – his tag still hadn't arrived before he left home, so they issued him a duplicate tag when he got to Idaho. My tag made it to my Post Office Box on August 12th. I wasn't terribly impressed with the lottery operation, but sometimes government employees take a year or two to figure things out. Evidently they hadn't gotten this one deciphered yet.

Before scouting the unit, we found a place to park my camp trailer. Since it would be brutally hot in the desert, it was suggested by several townspeople that we camp in a little county park next to a lake. Shade trees would offer relief from the burning August sun.

I found a nice little spot a few yards from the beach. Immediately I noticed some bathing beauties in the vicinity, and Nick and I had a devil of a time parking the rig. It had seemed so simple.

Our scouting efforts turned up some amazing information. The unit was quite large, stretching about 40 miles north and south, and 25 miles east and west. Most of it was hot, dry, sagebrush desert, but there were irrigated farmlands along the outer fringe of the unit.

The only mountains were a few hills sparsely covered with junipers, and a bunch of impressive sand dunes, some of them several hundred feet high.

We learned that the whole area was underlain with sand, bad sand that will immobilize your rig immediately if you're not careful. A solution was to use one of the little four-wheel outfits, but I don't have one of the rigs and relied instead on my 3/4 ton four-wheel drive Ford pickup, which was useless in the sand.

Zumbo says any successful elk hunt requires a certain amount of mental anguish.   photo by Nick Seifert

Though we drove about in the sagebrush looking for tracks, we saw nothing, not even an old bunch of droppings. Back in town, the locals were saying that all the elk had been killed off the year before. Nobody had seen a thing.

There was a unit just south of ours that also opened August 15, but very few permits were offered. Our unit had 300; the other had 50.

A number of good bulls had been spotted on a game management area in the other unit, and we were advised to concentrate our efforts along a county road that was the boundary of both units. Elk were commonly kicked off the south unit into ours.

Nick and I covered as much country in the truck as possible, simply looking for sign. We would have welcomed anything, even a one-week old track that proved an elk was alive and kicking in the unit, but we saw nothing.

It would have been useless to walk. It was a vast area and we'd waste too much time. Any elk in the area would have to cross one of the many roads. Locals told us that elk commonly traveled a dozen or more miles a day between hayfields and desert hideouts. It was impossible for them not to cross a road, if there indeed was an elk present. If they crossed a road they'd leave a track, and we'd see it. I hate driving around looking for sign, but we had no other options.

This was the most peculiar elk hunt I'd ever tackled. The temperature was scorching hot; Nick and I wore tee shirts. If we indeed got an elk, it was going to be a race of time to get it dressed, skinned, and to a cooler.

Residents told us elk bedded in tall sagebrush during the day. Nick and I looked at every thick patch of sage we came to, but nothing doing. In fact, the place was devoid of everything, not only elk. We saw no deer or antelope, and just a jackrabbit or cottontail now and then.

We had no idea where to begin hunting on opening morning. As we were headed back to camp, I stopped to get gasoline. At the station, a friendly UPS man told us he knew of a ranch where three bulls had been feeding. He showed us the ranch on a map, and we recognized the area as being close to where we'd scouted.

Since public land surrounded the ranch, Nick and I decided to try it in the morning. We had no reason to disbelieve the UPS man. Those folks are a fountain of knowledge. Little goes on that they don't know about. Unlike postmen who deliver to mailboxes in rural areas, the UPS carrier goes right to the house.

It was still dark when we drove through public land toward the ranch. Our plan was to park the truck and ease up toward the hayfield. We stayed put, thinking that spooked elk might head in our direction.

Nothing doing. An hour later we saw a motorhome and large camp trailer parked about 300 yards from the fields. Those hunters had erased any opportunity of anyone seeing an elk. No elk would visit the fields with strange vehicles parked that close.

Nick and I drove through the hot desert, looking for tracks, and at times we walked to look into promising cover. Nothing. There was not a single sign of an elk.

After several hours of aimless wandering, we returned to camp, only to find a bevy of beauties parading on the beach.

"Ever been in an elk camp like this before?" Nick laughed.

"It's pretty rugged all right," I answered. "Lots of mental anguish, eh Nick?"

After taking all the scenery we could stand, we headed back to the desert. This time I drove up on one of the sand dunes that was covered with brush. The road I traveled seemed hard, and there were plenty of tire tracks on it. We figured on driving out as far as we could, then parking the truck and walking.

Suddenly I felt the road go soft under the wheels. I stopped immediately, engaged the four-wheel drive, made a turn and crept out with steady power. I was most definitely not interested in being towed out by a wrecker.

Nick and I walked and drove, but still no sign of an elk. No other hunters had seen any elk either. We talked to every hunter we could. There weren't many; most were waiting for the general hunt to open. When it did, hundreds of elk would pour into the desert overnight, pushed there by hunters. The unit allowed either-sex the first month of the season; the second month it was cow-only. Of course, it went to cow-only before the place filled up with elk.

The second day we visited the ranch where the three bulls had allegedly visited. The rancher's wife was outside, and she told us there hadn't been a bull on the place for months. We chatted quite some time. She and her husband were avid hunters, and she said we should have been there last year.

"It was a war zone," she said. "There were elk and hunters everywhere. A lot of people got nice bulls."

We drove off, and I was absolutely confused.

"So much for our UPS guy," I sad, "and he had such an honest face."

Nick allowed as to how some people just couldn't be trusted, and we headed back to the miserable scorched desert.

That night we talked to our informant in town.

"A rancher stopped by my shop," he said. "Said three bulls have been hanging around off and on for weeks."

"Was it so and so?" I asked.

"Yep," the man said, "and he'll let you hunt. All you need to do is ask."

"He wouldn't be fibbing, would he?" I asked.

"Not a chance," the informant said. "He's as honest as they come."

Nick and I didn't know what to make of the situation. Did the rancher's wife tell us an outright lie, or was she unaware of the elk? I doubted the latter. If both of them were hunters, the husband no doubt would have told his wife. The little lady might have been telling us a little white lie.

We decided to see for ourselves. We went to the ranch (the lady

DID say we could hunt there) before daybreak the next morning, and staked it out. The campers had left, and there were no elk, either.

Nick and I walked down to the alfalfa field to check it out. Sure enough, much of the lush green field had been eaten by elk, but there was no fresh sign of feeding. The UPS man and rancher were right. Elk had been there all right, but there was no telling where they were now.

We hunted every conceivable place we could in the unit, and checked the ranch consistently. Still no elk. At one point, Nick and I climbed sand dunes to check the small groves of junipers on the sidehills.

Climbing a sand dune is quite an experience, one that I'm not interested in repeating again. If you know how difficult it is to walk in deep, soft sand along an ocean beach, consider the sand at a 30 percent grade.

It is sheer misery. You climb two feet and slide back one. Your boots sink deep in the sand, and you must yank them out to take another step.

And so it went for five days – walk the desert, drive, and hike the hills. And for five days we never saw a fresh elk track.

Nick left for the east coast without seeing an elk. The hunt was over for him, but since I live in Wyoming only a few hours away from the unit, I'm going back and collect a nice dry cow. As I write this, in the summer of 1990, I'm looking forward to returning to that dusty, sandy place when there's a few elk around.

Though we didn't get anything, Nick and I had a great hunt. There were lots of laughs, despite the frustrations. I can't tell you about the rattlesnake, because some snake lovers might get upset with me as to its fate. Suffice to say there is one less rattlesnake in Idaho.

For sure I'm staying away from that bikini-infested beach when I go back for my cow. But what the heck, when I'm laying in a snow-covered tent in some godforsaken wilderness and it's 20 below zero, I can always think about that little park with the shady trees and pretty girls.

Sometimes you just gotta be prepared for everything. I sure wish I'd have brought a bathing suit on that elk hunt . . . . .

BERTHA IS RETIRED

Reckon we could get Bushnell to put a scope on this baby for me Zumbo?!

(If this chapter seems familiar, you've probably read a similar version in OUTDOOR LIFE, or in my book, CALLING ALL ELK. In this chapter, however, I've revealed a couple of tidbits that weren't in the original story. Also, this hunt describes one of my finest all-time elk hunts, and I felt it was worth repeating).

At first, it had looked so easy, but now I was having profound second thoughts. The mountain was steeper than I had figured, and the sun was relentless. It wasn't supposed to be this hot in British Columbia during elk season.

Karl Schmidider and I kept climbing, easing our way cautiously up a razorback ridge that led to the mountaintop.

I peeled my shirts off and stuffed them into my daypack. Three hours before, I had shivered while riding a horse up the canyon, but now I was ready to shuck even the soaked T-shirt that clung to my skin.

It had been my idea to tie the horses and climb the mountain. There had been no special reason to do so, except to see what was on the other side. Our luck had been so bad that we were game for anything.

When we reached the summit, I lay down in the shade of a bush. Karl did likewise, and we relaxed as a freshening breeze occasionally wafted along and cooled the hot air.

If only Karl or I had had the good sense to carry a canteen, we would have been in better spirits. As it was, we cussed ourselves for our forgetfulness. The creek's soft gurgle far down in the canyon bottom didn't help, either. We were intensely thirsty. The air temperature was close to 90 degrees, and we had been climbing steadily for two hours.

I lay there with my head on my daypack, thinking about my parched mouth, when I noticed a large can on the ground several yards away.

"What's that big can doing up here in the middle of nowhere?" I asked Karl.

"Probably from Henry's sheep cache," Karl answered without moving. "This is where he sets up one of his spike camps."

Suddenly, Karl sat up and looked. Instantly, he was on his feet, and then I heard him grumble in his thick German accent. I vaguely made out a few choice unprintable words and something about grizzly bears.

I walked over to Karl, and saw the mess on the ridgetop. Cans, bottles and all sorts of food containers were scattered for 50 yards. A large metal drum—its contents gone—was lodged in some brush down the slope.

Karl pointed to the heavy stainless-steel cables that had once held the drum. The grizzly had not only ripped the drum from its cable moorings, but had also slashed open the heavy metal top, which had been tightly sealed.

Looking over the assortment of containers, I spotted a can of peaches still intact. I picked it up and immediately opened it with my knife. Karl declined my offer to share the peaches, but rummaged around and came up with a jug of water and more cans of fruit.

To the victor go the spoils, I thought, feeling like a coyote that cleans up on a grizzly kill. We indulged in the find, and later picked up most of the garbage and tossed it back into the drum.

"Henry will not be happy," Karl said, "but the bears are boss."

It was a simple statement, and having spent a great deal of time in grizzly country, I agreed.

With our thirst quenched, we lay down again, making small talk about bears, Canadians, Americans, world problems, women's rights and, naturally, elk hunting.

Karl, a German immigrant to Canada, guides for outfitter Henry Fercho in southeastern British Columbia's Kootenay Mountains. Karl and I had hit it off immediately, forming a fine relationship between hunter and guide. We understood each other perfectly, and I genuinely enjoyed his company. He was about 10 years older than I, and I liked his old-world European values and philosophy of life. Hunting with him was a pleasure, even though the weather had so far turned our elk efforts into futile ones.

The hunt had been organized by Bushnell/Bausch & Lomb to evaluate some new binoculars and riflescopes. Our party was made up of nine hunters, including General Chuck Yeager, former astronaut Joe Engle and hunting consultant Jack Atcheson, who had arranged the hunt. Henry had split us into three groups, with three hunters in each group. Mine included Yeager and Don Robertson, an executive with Bushnell.

Although we were hunting in September during the prime bugling season, the elk weren't cooperating because of the intense heat and extremely dry weather. I'd seen this happen before during hot weather, and wasn't surprised. Although elk will go about their breeding as usual under these conditions, they're far less vocal and less likely to respond to calling.

Neither Don, Chuck nor I had heard an elk bugle during the first three days, though we had hunted hard and had never seen camp in the daylight.

On the first day, Yeager had killed a black bear with an unbelievable single shot at 450 yards. More than anything, he had wanted to give his first grandson a bear rug for Christmas. The salted bear pelt in camp had given us all a bit of encouragement.

Yeager's bear did not come without incident, however. Chuck had rested his rifle on a rock, drawn a steady bead, and squeezed the trigger of his mighty .300 Weatherby Magnum. Because he was so relaxed when he pressed the trigger, the riflescope belted him solidly, and he received a nasty scope cut over his eye.

Pain and blood was nothing for the General, who has been in his share of accidents after a lifetime of combat fighting over enemy skies and as a test pilot for the Air Force. He came into camp that night with blood on his forehead, and the familiar Yeager grin.

After Karl and I spent another hour at the cache wrecked by the grizzly, we walked (slid would be a better word for it) off the steep mountain to our horses. Karl figured that it would be a good idea to hunt the higher country. Henry has more than a dozen elk camps in his vast hunting unit—all are very comfortable cabins accessible by horses. We headed back to camp to have a "round table" with the other guides.

Yeager, Robertson and their guides rode into camp during

midday. After a brief discussion, there was a unanimous decision to move up to a camp in a glacial cirque. When we learned that a fine mountain lake loaded with cutthroat trout was just a few yards from the cabin, Yeager's eyes lit up.

"Let's go," he said. "I just happen to have a pack rod in my duffle. We can share it."

After we packed our gear, Yeager and I stood near the cabin and talked about elk. Suddenly, a gust of wind blew through the trees, shaking hundreds of brilliantly hued aspen leaves from their branches.

"What a beautiful sight," Yeager said as the bright leaves spun delicately to the forest floor. "That's what hunting is all about. Just seeing the natural beauty in this wilderness is worth it."

This was not my first trip with Chuck Yeager, so his eloquent remarks didn't surprise me. But to many people who know Yeager as a tough, fearless fighter pilot who knocked down five German warplanes in one day, or as a test pilot who still flies brand-new jets, or as a retired general who is a former director of safety for the U.S. Air Force, those comments would perhaps have raised a few eyebrows.

The truth is that Chuck Yeager was all of the above at one time or another, and through it all, he has never lost his intense love of the outdoors no matter where in the world he has traveled. After a half-dozen hunting and fishing trips with Yeager, I know him as one of the most ardent, avid outdoorsmen I have ever been acquainted with.

In addition, the man is good. Whether he's casting a dry fly for a cagey rainbow trout, or hitting a squirrel in the eye with a .22 bullet, or skillfully battling a 50-pound king salmon, he's good.

Yeager says that one of the reasons why he survived World War II was because of the woodlore skills he had learned while growing up in rural West Virginia. When his airplane was shot down over German-occupied France, he managed to escape through snowy mountains while dragging a wounded buddy.

Yeager's oldest son, Don, told me of several close calls in Vietnam when he had survived only because his Dad had taught him how to live in the outdoors.

As we rode along the trail to the higher elk camp, a grouse jumped up on a log and eyed us curiously. Yeager dismounted immediately and looked for rocks on the ground. We all knew his intentions when we saw the slingshot.

Two minutes and four shots later, Yeager walked back to the trail with four grouse in his hand.

"Here's dinner, boys," he said with a wide grin. "Now, let's catch some trout to go with the birds."

We had barely arrived in camp when Yeager rushed to the lake with his rod and assortment of shrimp-pattern flies that had been tied by his son, Mickey. A half-hour later, he returned to the cabin and handed me his Loomis rod.

"Your turn," he said. "I'll clean these fish, and you bring me some more."

I wasted no time getting to the water. I was eager to add some trout to the frying pan, but I was also anxious to have a General clean my fish. At that moment, elk hunting was far from top priority.

We had a splendid dinner that evening and talked about the new strategy for the morning, which was to walk from the cabin to prime areas and try bugling.

Despite our efforts the next day, the elk didn't respond favorably. We all heard bulls bugle, but the animals were entrenched in extremely dense timber. No matter what we tried, the bulls were uninterested.

Other animals, however, kept us amused while the elk were uncooperative. We saw plenty of bighorn sheep, moose, and both black and grizzly bears. One afternoon, Karl and I saw six black bears and a grizzly feeding on a slope that was blanketed with lush berry patches. Though I had a black bear tag, I didn't intend to try for a bear until I had first taken a bull elk.

Karl and I did work a bull in a basin on the seventh and eighth mornings, but the bull bugled a dozen times or so before eventually melting farther into the forest. I heard cows in his vicinity, and knew we were working a herd bull. He was acting routinely. Karl's bugle calls merely prompted the bull to gather up his girls and move away from us. The elk didn't want a confrontation with another bull.

When the same bull answered our call on the ninth morning, I suggested to Karl that we try something different. I left Karl at our vantage point to continue bugling occasionally while I eased about 150 yards down the slope.

I found a good position and blew a cow call. By that time, the bull had quit responding to Karl's bugle, as he'd done the previous two mornings. When there was no answer to my call, I waited five minutes and blew it again. Still, there was no answer, so I waited ten minutes and tried once more. After giving the bull another 10 minutes, I decided that he wasn't going to show, and climbed back up the mountain toward Karl.

I was about 10 yards from Karl when he pointed down into the basin. I turned to see a respectable six-point bull silently walking toward my former position. Cussing myself for leaving, I made a quick decision after studying the bull. The wind had begun to swirl, and the bull had changed his direction of travel, heading back into the timber from where he had come.

There was no question this was the herd bull that we'd played with for two days. He was intimidated by Karl's bugle challenge, but he responded to the cow call.

The shot would be around 350 yards. Had I stayed where I was when I had used the cow call, the bull would have been only 200 yards out.

But there was no time to lament. I found a solid rest for my .30/06, and figured the elevation for the distance. I didn't like having to shoot that far, but I was confident in my rifle as well as the new 2.5X-to-10X Bausch & Lomb scope that topped it.

The elk was standing broadside at the first shot, and I knew that the bullet had hit low. Instead of running, however, the bull took a step and looked around, confused by the echo of the shot in the basin. The next shot was also low, and the bull walked rapidly toward a pocket of heavy timber.

Now I was upset with myself because I was questioning my rifle's performance. At that point, though, I realized that the bull was probably much farther away than I'd originally figured. The elk slowed momentarily to step over a log, and I raised the crosshairs a full 14 inches. At the shot, the bull faltered momentarily and ran into the timber.

Sitting quietly after the last shot, I heard a thump in the forest that sounded like a big animal falling heavily to the ground. The wind had been perfectly calm at that point, enabling me to hear for a long distance.

I was confident that I'd hit the elk, but Karl wasn't so sure. He hadn't seen the elk when I'd shot the third time, and he hadn't heard the thump because he had been walking through brush down toward me.

"Long shot," Karl said, almost apologetically.

"Real long," I answered. "A lot farther than I figured, but I believe he's down."

With no further discussion, we worked our way down to where the bull had stood when I had shot at him. I found the exact spot where the elk had been stepping when I'd fired, but found no trace of blood. There was a set of deep hoofprints where the bull had lunged after the shot, but the dry ground revealed no more tracks.

Karl and I searched for a full hour in vain. There was not a speck of blood, and I was starting to lose my former confidence.

"You really think you hit him?" Karl asked.

"I don't know what to think," I answered. "I was sure I heard him fall, and I saw him stagger when I shot, but now I'm not at all sure."

We searched some more, but still found no evidence of the blood or hair that would signify a hit.

What happened next still makes me shudder when I think about it.

"I don't think he's hit," Karl said, "but we'll keep on looking if you want to."

"I'm beginning to think you're right," I said. "Let's try once more, and then head for camp if we don't find anything."

Again we looked, this time covering more area in the very dense forest. We made large circles, moving slowly and calling out to each other so that we could look methodically.

Finally, when it seemed that we had done everything humanly possible to find the elk, I convinced myself that I'd missed. I'd crawled around on my hands and knees so much, looking for the tiniest pinhead of blood, that my knees ached.

"Let's go," I said. "I missed."

As I turned to leave, I wondered what Chuck Yeager would think back at camp. It's no sin to miss, after all, and I had done it before, but I felt as though I'd let Karl, Henry, the Bushnell people and the rest of our party down.

But as we were climbing out of the basin, I had a powerful sense of recall that made me stop in my tracks. In my mind, I reenacted the precise moment of the shot, and I clearly saw the elk falter. He hadn't simply slipped or stumbled—he had reacted to the impact of the bullet. Just as clearly, I heard the thump over and over.

Suddenly, I knew that the elk was dead. There was no question about it.

"I'll meet you back at camp, Karl," I said. "I want to try one more time."

Karl looked at me incredulously. "I'll go with you," he said.

"It will only take me a few minutes," I answered. "That bull is dead. Wait here, and I'll call you."

I ran back down the mountain like a crazy man. It mattered no longer that there was no blood. This had happened to me before, even while bowhunting and making a fatal hit with an arrow. Blood doesn't have to be present.

When I reached the area, I walked confidently to the spot where

I had seen the bull falter—the same spot that Karl and I had searched several times. A strange force was guiding me onward. I felt goose bumps crawling around on the back of my neck and my arms, and I knew the elk was close.

Incredibly, I spotted the bull lying in a small gully that was surrounded by a tight cluster of spruce trees. He'd lunged into a depression that had contained his body perfectly, and he had died with his belly to the ground, his back to the sky and his legs folded beneath him. His pelt blended perfectly with the sun-dappled underbrush, and his antlers were shrouded by low branches of thick spruces.

I waited a moment before calling Karl, as I was overwhelmed with emotion, reflecting on the tragedy that had almost occurred.

Karl and I field-dressed the bull, and I noted that the Remington Core-Lokt bullet had penetrated the bottom half of each lung. The elk had run 85 yards from where I had hit him.

Chuck Yeager returned with Karl and me and the other two guides later that afternoon to pack out the bull. When I showed Yeager where the bull had stood when I had hit him and the mountain slope from where I had fired, he let out a low whistle. "No wonder you shot three times," he said, smiling. "You must have been zeroing in on that bull artillery fashion. If you'd been using my .300 Weatherby Mag, you'd have dropped that old boy in his tracks."

Yeager had a twinkle in his eye as we walked to the bull. As we approached the elk, Yeager broke off the end of a spruce twig that was shaped like a cross. He dipped it in the elk's blood and then grasped my hand in a firm handshake. Yeager spoke in German and told me what to say in response. I repeated after him, and he translated afterward, explaining that the ceremony was a ritual performed in Germany to show reverence to the elk as well as to the hunter.

I was moved by Yeager's genuine respect for the dead bull. The jet pilot had a lot of class, as well as affection and reverence for wild things.

Yeager left our party early, heading for camp at a trot. I wondered why he had left so soon, but I found out why later.

Just before dinner, everyone in our group was gathered outside the cabin, and I noted some whispering here and there. Yeager walked up to me with a grin on his face and held out his .300 Weatherby Magnum.

"If you'll retire Bertha," he said, "you can have this rifle."

I looked at Bertha, my Winchester Model 70 that I had hunted with faithfully for 25 years, and looked back at Yeager. I was dumbfounded—at a loss for words—which is unusual for me.

"Are you serious?" I replied.

Yeager nodded, the grin even wider.

"Suppose I don't retire her, but give her to my son?" I asked. I had been considering that possibility for the last couple of years, anyway.

"It's a deal," Yeager responded. "Next time you shoot at an elk 400 yards away, use this .300. Here's what it did at 200 yards when you were packing out the bull."

Yeager showed me a paper plate with three holes punched neatly in the middle. He had left us and the bull early so that he could make sure the rifle was dead on before giving it to me.

The next Christmas, my son, Danny, opened up a long box to see a well-used Winchester with a red ribbon tied around the barrel. He looked at me and didn't have to say a word to show his love and gratitude.

As we hugged, I recalled fond memories when Danny had traipsed after me dozens of times as I hunted with Bertha. He had been at my side on many occasions when I had taken deer, elk, and antelope with the old rifle, and I remembered when, at age 12, Danny had fired the .30/06 for the first time. It had been a milestone, and I had seen how proud he had been as he blew at the blue smoke curling from the barrel.

When Danny graduated from college, we were saying our goodbyes before he headed off to California, where he'd start a new job with an aircraft firm in aerospace technology.

"By the way, Dad," he said, "forgot to tell you, but I was varmint hunting with Bertha last week. Shot three rockchucks at 300 yards each, and all in the head."

The kid really knew how to hurt a guy. I smiled as valiantly as I could, all the time mentally thanking Chuck Yeager for giving me the reason to share Bertha with my boy.

Next year, by the way, Danny and I will be hunting together in Wyoming. Bertha still has plenty of straight shots left in her, and when Danny kills his bull, I'm going to look for a spruce twig shaped like a cross and teach him a wonderful custom that I learned high on a mountain in British Columbia.

Thanks again, Chuck.

A TOUGH CHOICE

The bull elk wasn't much to write home about, but he was nonetheless a worthy quarry. It was the last day of the season, and the small four-pointer would fill my winter's meat requirement.

I had just climbed a steep hill and was out of breath. With luck, the elk would stay put until I'd calmed down enough to draw a steady bead.

It wasn't meant to be. When he started walking from the opening toward the timber, I quickly dropped to a sitting position and centered the scope on the bull's chest.

Though I was breathing hard, I was confident I could settle down momentarily for the shot. Drawing a deep breath, I squeezed the trigger and felt the sharp recoil of the rifle against my shoulder.

The bull humped up when the bullet hit, and made a quick dash to the timber. I knew instantly that the projectile wasn't on the course I wanted. The sight picture showed that at the moment I fired, the reticle was a touch too far back on the elk's body. I had a nagging feeling that I'd hit him in the paunch.

When I arrived at the spot the elk was standing, particles of intestine documented my worst fears. He was gutshot.

The ground was dry, and I knew I was in for a tough challenge. I had six hours of daylight to find the bull.

The rest of the day was a time of frustration and despair. I cussed myself for shooting, but then, hunting is an imperfect activity. I tried to reassure myself that sometimes it was necessary to make a shot when conditions aren't quite right, but those words of consolation wouldn't help me find the bull.

I'd followed his trail for at least a mile, working from one crimson speck to another. Finally, I lost his trail completely. No matter how hard I tried, I couldn't locate his route.

I left the last spot of blood and made ever-widening circles in the timber. All I could hope for was to stumble into the dead bull, or possibly flush him from his bed and make a killing shot. With 20 minutes of light left, I had just about given up. The dreaded feeling of wounding and losing an animal washed through me, and I was badly upset.

Suddenly I heard a branch crack, and then another. A large animal or human was walking in the timber.

Hoping it was my wounded bull, I found an elevated vantage spot and watched. The animal that walked into sight almost took my breath away. A superb bull strode along, carrying six points on each antler. His royal points and brow tines appeared to be at least 20 inches long, and his rack was wide. I knew from a quick glance that he'd score at least 325. At that point in time, he was the biggest bull I'd ever seen in the woods.

The bull was only 60 yards away, offering me the perfect shot that I didn't have on the smaller bull I'd wounded. I raised my rifle. But I couldn't shoot. Nagging thoughts of the gutshot bull evoked powerful feelings. Legally I'd done everything possible to find the small bull, and I'd have been justified to shoot the huge bull in front of me. For all I knew, the wounded bull might have recovered.

My attempt at rationalizing was a failure. No way could I shoot this giant bull, and I watched painfully as he disappeared in the timber.

It was almost dark, and my last attempt at finding my bull failed.

While driving out that evening, I passed a hunting camp and spotted some people hanging a bull in a tree. I stopped to help, and in the lantern light noted the bull looked similar to mine.

"We didn't shoot this bull," the hunter said. "Found him dead with a bullet in his paunch. He was still warm, so I tagged him. He's a fine piece of meat."

Further conversation indicated they'd located the bull about a half mile from where I'd lost his trail and only 50 yards from a road.

I had a cup of coffee with the men, and headed home. A cold wind came up, and snow flurries sliced in from an approaching storm. It would be a long drive home, in more ways than just the distance.

A TIME FOR WARM MITTENS

Gary Duffy rode through the timber ahead of me, moving at a good clip. Our horses walked briskly along a trail etched in the Montana forest, headed for an area that Gary figured would hold elk.

Darkness was just 20 minutes away when Gary dismounted and tied his horse to a tree. I did likewise, and quickly pulled my rifle from the scabbard. We wasted no time walking through the timber, toward the place Gary wanted to look at.

Presently I saw an opening ahead, a windswept ridge bordered by a three foot snowbank. We eased through the soft powder deposited by strong winds, and crept to the top.

Moments later, we spotted animals on the slope below us. A dozen elk had their heads down, hungrily feeding on the frozen yellow grass exposed by the wind. A quick look revealed two bulls, neither of them very interesting.

"We can do a whole lot better," Gary said. "Let's watch the edge of the timber until shooting light is over. There are some big bulls in here."

Our vigil was unrewarding. A few bighorn sheep appeared, but the bull I was looking for didn't show.

It was dark when Gary and I arrived at the corral. We made plans to meet before dawn the next day.

I was confident about the hunt's outcome for several reasons. Gary is a competent outfitter working in superb country for big bulls, and there was a generous blanket of snow on the ground.

Snow, in my estimation, is an extraordinary ingredient that works magic where elk live. Snow inundates feed in the high country, forcing elk to lower elevations. Because elk must migrate to survive when snow piles high, they place themselves into a vulnerable position when they're evicted from the upper contours and into areas more accessible to hunters. Furthermore, snow allows elk to be seen more readily at long distances, and it also offers tracking opportunities.

Gary's area is close to Yellowstone Park, which gave me even more reason to be confident. Not only do resident elk herds in his territory have big bulls, but there was always a good chance that Yellowstone's bulls would move into his hunting area.

The hunt began with my good pal, Jack Atcheson Sr., a resident of Butte, Montana and one of the best big game hunters I know. Atcheson is a hunting consultant, and accompanied Jack O'Connor on several hunts. Atcheson and I were hunting on our own, hiking afoot in the deep snow. The spot we hunted was just a few miles from Duffy's ranch.

One evening, Gary Duffy drove up and invited us to hunt with him. He had horses, as well as some good spots to hunt. Atcheson and Duffy have been good friends for years, and Jack wasted no time accepting Gary's invitation. The outfitter is an affable man, with a wide grin and a firm handshake. He had a fine reputation for producing big elk, and I was delighted at the opportunity to hunt with him.

The next morning, Gary, Jack, and I hiked up a mountain long before daybreak. The trees cast eerie shadows in the moonlight, and

One of my best bulls ever – late in the season is my favorite time – this is proof

we found our way without flashlights. After walking 45 minutes in very cold temperatures, Gary pointed to an open knoll in the timber, which offered a good look at much of the country below.

"Stand right there and keep your eyes peeled," Gary advised. "This is a great elk crossing, and that opening offers a good look at some excellent country."

Jack agreed, having killed a big bull in the same general area a few years ago. I made my way to the knoll while Jack headed off for a vantage point across the ridge. Gary left to do some scouting, checking tracks in the snow.

The temperature was not much above zero, which was typical for the middle of November in Montana. I wasn't uncomfortable during the vigil, but I can't say I was toasty warm when I walked down off the mountain several hours later after an uneventful watch. I'd learned a long time ago that a bit of suffering was involved during late season elk hunts.

That afternoon, Gary and I rode horses to the windswept ridge I mentioned at the beginning of the article, while Jack stillhunted.

It was just as cold the next morning when we walked back up the mountain. I had just settled myself and adjusted my heavy mittens when three big bulls appeared from the timber. They stopped momentarily in a small area of sparse brush, looked at me, and suddenly bolted into the trees.

I jerked my mittens off, fired at the biggest bull, and in a few minutes Gary and I admired the elk. He was one of my best, scoring 343 Boone and Crockett points.

Gary hiked back to the ranch for horses to pack out the bull, while Jack tracked the other two elk. He was unsuccessful, but returned a couple days later to kill a bull about as big as mine.

Late season elk hunting often ends on a happy note such as ours. Most of my best bulls have come at the tag end of the season, when many hunters have oiled their guns and put them away.

Hunters who try for elk as late in the year as possible are less apt to say to heck with elk hunting. A bit of pain and suffering are often involved, but that's what elk hunting is all about. Sometimes a LOT of pain and suffering are required, but that's often necessary to put your tag on a bull. I guess it's all part of a day's work.

THE DAY BIG ERNIE SMILED

I tell ya there ain't no damn elk up here!

Most astute elk hunters know that Alberta, Canada has produced some mighty big bulls. In fact, in 1977, a farmer by the name of Clarence Brown achieved instant recognition among elk hunters when he killed a giant bull that scored 419 3/8. Clarence's bull was the biggest ever taken in the 20th century, and after news of his elk was made known, Alberta suddenly became the place to go for monster bulls.

I was feeling sorry for myself for several years because I hadn't had an opportunity to hunt in Alberta. My chance came in 1986 when the boys from the Rocky Mountain Elk Foundation asked me if I'd be interested in going on an all-expenses paid hunt in Alberta. The Foundation planned to use the hunt as incentive for a membership drive. The winner of the contest would get to go with me on the hunt.

It took me less than 1/2 of a second to agree on the deal. The hunt was planned for the last week of the Alberta season which happened to be late November, and also happened to be Thanksgiving week in the U.S. (Canadians celebrate their Thanksgiving in October).

The hunt was planned as late as possible because we hoped for a shot at one of the huge bulls that migrate out of Banff National Park and into the area we'd be hunting. (Make that Two Shots — one for the winner of the contest and one for me)

As it turned out, Steve Ferguson from Georgia won the contest. The hunt was on, and to say I was not excited would be a gross lie.

I flew to Calgary and was met by Pat Bates, who runs Storm Mountain Outfitters. I didn't know it at the time, but Pat had set me up for a great practical joke.

After I went through customs in the Calgary Airport, Pat and I walked into the lobby toward a small group of people. A couple of them had video cameras aimed at us.

Pat introduced me to a very large man in the group, and identified him as Steve Ferguson. As I shook the man's hand, I wondered how he'd ever get on a horse, or even if Pat had a big enough horse to hold him. I had immediate vibes that Steve would be lucky to get a bull, much less get to camp.

As we headed for the exit of the airport, another man walked over and held out his hand. He had a big grin on his face when he said, "Hi Jim, I'm Steve Ferguson."

The boys and I had a grand laugh over the joke, and I knew at that moment that this was going to be a great hunt. The big man who posed as Steve was a friend of Pat's, and laughed heartily with the rest of us.

Steve and I had dinner at Pat's house that night and later checked into a motel. The next morning a bunch of us loaded into pickup trucks, and we headed for the hunting area which was a few hours drive from Calgary.

On the way up, Pat informed Steve and I that we needed super cold temperature and deep snow to move elk out of Banff National Park. Up to that point, there was only six inches of snow on the ground and it hadn't been very cold.

A light snow fell as we drove, and we hoped it would pile up deep. When we hit the end of the paved highway, we stopped at a junction affectionately known as Beverage Corners. In order to live up to its name, we parked the trucks along the road, and had a brief refreshment. With that accomplished, we had a short drive down the dirt road, and arrived at the trail head on the banks of the Red Deer River.

The place was bustling with hunters heading into the forest or coming out. I noted with satisfaction a guide leading several pack horses, two of which carried enormous sets of elk antlers. The guide and his pack train formed an eerie sight, as they rode down the trail in dense fog and swirling snowflakes.

The trail was not really a trail at all but an old road that had been closed to vehicle traffic years ago by the Wildlife Department. However, Canadian hunters used their ingenuity and came up with a nifty solution. Rather than hauling gear in on pack horses, they built wagons pulled by a team of horses, just like the old conestoga wagons that were used to settle the west. Pat's rig was a sharp looking outfit, painted fire engine red with a white cloth top (Pat, incidentally, is a fireman in Calgary).

After packing the wagon, we headed up the road on saddle horses, while Pat commandeered the wagon. All in all, there were about ten hunters and guides. All of the hunters were locals from the Calgary area except Steve and I.

Camp consisted of a huge tent which would sleep all of us as well as serve as the kitchen and dining area. What caught my eye right away was the unique outhouse which had an infrared heat lamp plugged into the camp generator. It was the first time I'd ever been in a backcountry camp with the luxury of sitting on a warm toilet seat. Right then I decided that Pat and Mike had a touch of class.

Since there's no Sunday hunting in Alberta and we arrived in camp on Sunday afternoon, we hung around and glassed the mountain slopes for elk. We saw a couple herds but they included cows, calves, and spike bulls. In the unit we hunted, a legal bull had to have at least five points on each side.

After a superb meal, we went to bed or, I should say, tried to go to bed. Our sleeping arrangements were such that a bunch of foam cushions were laid side by side along one wall of the tent. Imagine if you will, a dozen grown men trying to sleep when a few irascible individuals, especially the wild man we had as our cook, insisted on telling bad jokes. There were plenty of giggles, snores, and other unmentionable noises caused by the cook who had fiendishly concocted bean soup for dinner.

Pat Bates wasted no time getting ready in the morning. At 3:30

Steve Ferguson and I with his giant Alberta bull. Steve had first shot, and the elk won RMEF's Bull Of The Woods contest.

sharp, he and the other guides were outside saddling horses. By 4:45, we were horseback heading out for Alberta's giant bulls.

At this point I should mention that our hunting unit included the very spot where Clarence Brown killed the record bull in 1977. That fact, plus the publicity by the Elk Foundation on the hunt with Steve Ferguson and I, contributed to the area being a popular spot to hunt elk.

As we soon learned, there were hunters everywhere, and to add further to the confusion, outfitters could hunt anywhere they wished without being assigned specific territories.

The area we hunted was crown land managed by the government as public land similar to national forests in the United States. Banff National Park lay about a dozen miles to our west. The strategy was to hunt elk moving east out of the park, which forbids hunting, and onto government lands just east of the boundary. Old roads had been cut through the timber of the mountains we hunted, serving as good trails for our saddle horses.

Pat, Steve, and I rode for about 25 miles that day and saw about 50 elk — all of them cows, calves, and small bulls. Unfortunately, the snow had quit and the weather was around zero. Pat wasn't happy with the conditions, but I learned a long time ago that there's nothing you can do about the weather. Ma nature always gets the last laugh.

The next day was more of the same. We rode horseback, checking for fresh tracks in the snow, and glassing for elk on windblown ridges. We saw more cows and calves and small bulls, but the big boys we wanted were so far being elusive.

For our lunch break, we tied our horses and settled into the snow to eat sandwiches.

"She don't look too good, fellers," Pat announced.

"You aren't being pessimistic already, are you Patrick?" I said. "This is only our second day."

"Too many hunters," Pat responded, "and the weather isn't what I wanted. It'll take a miracle to move those big bulls around."

When we finished eating I noted that the wind had picked up considerably. We kept riding higher and higher, until we reached the top of a mountain. Pat explained that a windswept ridge was a good spot to look for big bulls at the end of the day.

To get to the spot, we had to ride out of the timber and into the opening where the wind was now gusting furiously.

"Looks like a fullblown hurricane out there to me, Pat" I said, as I looked from the sheltered forest onto the bare mountaintop.

"Just a little breeze," Pat responded with a grin. "Remember, this is elk hunting."

At that, we rode out of the timber where we had to cross a drift of powdered snow about four feet high.

Pat went first and his horse immediately bogged down in the snow. He urged the horse onward and the animal leaped and bucked to plow through the drift. The rest of us followed and our horses immediately succumbed to the depths of the snow.

Amidst all of the confusion, the wind whipped up the snow that was being churned by the horses, reducing visibility to almost zero. I was barely able to open my eyes in the incredibly driven wind and snow, and all I could see was a crazy scene of panicky horses and snowcovered humans.

I'll never forget what one of the other hunters who was from

The Bates brothers use a unique transportation system to get to elk camp.

Alberta said to me.

"This is Canadian!" he shouted above the deafening roar of the wind, "I love it!"

This was one tough guy, I thought, or else a little bit crazy.

Somehow we made it through the drift onto the opening that was blown free of snow. The opening, however, presented other problems. The full force of the gale ripped into us. It was impossible to breathe unless you turned your head away from the wind, and even at that, you had to gasp for air.

Undeterred, Pat kept going and we rode out on the ridge working our way higher to where we could see off to the other side. The wind was even worse when we topped out. It was so bad that our horses were literally being forced along by the powerful gusts. I finally dismounted and walked on the leeward side of the horse for relief.

Even though I was properly clothed with full winter gear, it was no match for the fury of the storm. I wore thermal longjohns, heavy woolen trousers, and plenty of socks, shirts, jackets, and gloves.

Pat kept heading for the very top where we could peek over. He was also walking along the leeward side of his horse, as was the rest of our party. The horses lurched about as the wind pushed them around, and we did our best to stay on their protected side.

"We got to look over this ridge," he yelled.

He tried to say something else but the wind sucked his breath away. Mercifully, Pat walked over to the edge, took a quick look and turned back.

"To heck with elk hunting," he yelled.

"We all agree," I screamed back, speaking for the rest of the party. I was unsure if Pat heard me over the three foot distance that separated us.

We eventually gained the security of the timber, and the difference was like night and day. Regular breathing was resumed, and it appeared that we weren't going to die after all. In all my years of elk hunting, camp never looked so good. We learned later from a portable radio, that the wind had been gusting up to 100 miles per hour in the area we'd been hunting. I never did check to see what the wind chill factor was. I guess I didn't want to know.

The next day, Steve, Pat, and I stillhunted through some sparsely vegetated country where elk often fed. Pat didn't want to stir animals up in the thick timber for fear of running them out of the country. The strategy was to look for animals feeding naturally in openings. Again we saw no legal bulls.

The forth day was Thanksgiving. When we arose at 3:30, Pat asked Steve and I if we were willing to ride long and hard. I'd ridden long and hard lots of times, but today was to be the grand champion of all my long and hard riding hunts. Before it was over, we'd travel 45 miles on horseback.

We skipped breakfast, and were in the frost-covered saddles by 4:00. By daybreak we'd already ridden 12 miles.

We had to cross the Panther River, and I wasn't much liking the requirement of riding the horse on a shelf of ice to the edge of the water, jumping the horse into the bitterly cold river, riding across, and jumping on the shelf of ice on the other side. One slip into the water would be fatal. Huge chunks of ice flowed downstream, disappearing into a black hole under the river below that was completely frozen over. It didn't take a genius to recognize that a man caught in the current would be sucked under the ice downriver.

Pat went first, and I followed with Steve behind me. Lots of thoughts went through my mind as my horse walked across the treacherous ice toward the river. I vaguely remember wondering if a big bull elk was really worth it, but the crossing was uneventful. Nonetheless, I'll never forget my feelings when I crossed that river.

We rode nonstop the rest of the day, pausing only to look for feeding elk and tracks in the snow. We rode past Clarence Brown's camp, and Pat showed me the precise spot where Clarence had killed the third biggest elk in the world.

At one point we stopped at a camp to chat with a woman whose husband was out hunting. She invited us in for coffee, and I'll always

Canadians are ingenious sometimes. A heat lamp in this outhouse resulted in a warm toilet seat – quite a luxury in elk camp.

remember the fresh bannock she gave us. Bannock is a simple bread made in the North country - somewhat bland tasting, but delicious in its own way.

As we rode back in the dark to camp, Pat called out for us to listen. Steve and I halted our horses, and in the distance we heard the unmistakable sound of two bighorn rams clashing their horns together. It sounded like a cue ball hitting another ball on a pool table, and we listened for several minutes. It was one of those moments that will be etched forever in my memory bank. Every now and then I recall that moment and hear those big rams battling under the star-studded, icy Canadian sky.

We arrived in camp at 9:00 and walked to a neighboring camp where we'd been invited for Thanksgiving dinner. The outfitter's tent held 42 people, and we were treated to a traditional Thanksgiving meal of turkey and all the trimmings.

I managed to eat, even though I was bone weary from more than 15 hours in the saddle.

On Friday, the fifth day of the hunt, we rode several miles and stillhunted likely places. During our lunch break, we sat in a small copse of trees. Pat looked forlorn and threw a snowball down the mountain.

"She's looking ugly," he exclaimed.

If I hadn't known some of Pat's sayings, I'd have asked who was looking ugly, but I knew what he meant. The hunt was looking bad.

"Any suggestions?" I asked.

"Just a dumb one," Pat answered. "There's a muskeg bottom near camp that big elk tracks have been seen in. The boys have been looking it over pretty hard, but the elk are coming out at night to feed. I've looked at every chunk of land in this area and I think big bulls are pretty scarce. Let's try that spot near camp."

We rode to camp, turned our horses loose in the corral, and walked about half a mile to the muskeg bottom. We found a vantage point where we could see most of the meadow, and settled down to wait.

"I had a talk with Big Ernie last night," Pat said, "and told him I needed a little help."

"Is Ernie up there," I exclaimed, pointing up to the sky.

"Yup," Pat replied. "We need lots of help."

I could understand Pat's dejected feelings. This hunt had been highly touted by the Elk Foundation. The entire membership was waiting for the outcome. Not only was Pat's reputation at stake, but his pride as well. Some day he had hoped to retire from the fire department and be a full-time outfitter. If our hunt was successful, he'd have plenty of credibility toward his goal.

There was about a half hour of shooting light left when Pat made a startling announcement.

"There's a bull!" he said. "Three bulls," he added correcting himself. "One of them is huge."

I couldn't believe what I saw. A giant bull was strutting out of the timber, followed by two other smaller bulls. If one of those smaller bulls was by himself, he would be a trophy in his own right, but they were overshadowed by the giant.

I had told Steve at the beginning of the hunt, that rather than flipping a coin if one good bull showed up, he would have the shot. He won the contest, and I thought it was only fair that he had the first opportunity.

Steve drew a bead on the big bull, and I lay down in the snow, centering my scope on the bigger of the other two. The one I chose looked fairly heavy and had seven points on one side and six on the other.

The bulls were about 400 yards out, which was about as far as I like to shoot, but I had no choice.

As soon as Steve fired, the other two bulls stood still and looked around for the source of the shot. I touched the trigger and saw the bull stagger. I fired again and he walked 30 yards, fell over and lay still. Steve's big bull was hit hard and had run into the timber.

With darkness coming on rapidly, we ran toward the elk. When I saw that mine was dead, I ran over towards Steve and Pat to help them locate Steve's bull. We didn't have very far to go, and found him lying dead about 200 yards from mine.

After a brief series of handshakes and backslaps, I ran over to dress my bull while Pat dressed Steve's. We had the chores done just as it was too dark to see.

Camp was buzzing with excitement that night. The other hunters were about as happy as Steve, Pat and I were, and we managed to eliminate some of the fine Canadian liquid that we had in camp.

We returned to the bulls the next day, which would have been the last day of the hunt. After posing for pictures and quartering the elk, Pat and I sat down on a stump .

"Do you realize the odds of us killing those two bulls?" I said to Pat.

The weather was uncooperative, and none of the fifty hunters in the valley saw a legal bull during the week of hunting. We had simply walked out a half a mile from camp and watched the place that dozens of other hunters had watched all week. Those three bulls walked right out, just like it was somehow planned.

"I told you I had a talk with Big Ernie," Pat reminded me. "I figger that maybe we had a little miracle working for us."

"Amen, old buddy," I said. "Amen."

(NOTE. We learned later that Steve's bull scored around 362 Boone and Crockett points, winning the Elk Foundation's Bull Of The Woods Contest.)

SHOWTIME IN THE ELK WOODS

Maaake - up!

I've never said to heck with elk hunting and really meant it, though there have been times when I was ready to throw in the towel. On the other hand, I've said to heck with video hunts, because they are so frustrating that they make me a little crazy.

Consider this: When you're doing a hunting video, you're under enormous pressure to perform. When it comes time to shoot an animal, it must be done tastefully, the light must be right, the sound must be correct, the animal must be humanely taken, the animal and hunter should both be in view when the shot is made, and the quarry should be in focus.

If that isn't demanding, then I don't know what is. Furthermore, all other aspects of the production sometimes require herculean efforts, such as packing hundreds of pounds of gear around, keeping video camera batteries warm when it's 20 degrees below zero, and figuring out a good script. Being somewhat of an actor is also a requirement.

I've done four hunting videos for three different companies. One was on bighorn sheep, another on mule deer, and two on elk.

The sheep video was done in Wyoming's high country adjacent to Yellowstone Park. We had a crew of four, including me, outfitter Nate Vance, and the two cameramen.

To get to the hunting area, we had to ride 34 miles on horses to get to Nate's base camp, and then another nine miles to the spike camp. Besides our regular hunting gear and personal items, we had four pack mules loaded to the gills with video gear.

Making matters worse was the fact that sheep camp was in the area where Yellowstone Park rangers drop troublesome grizzlies. These bad actors are captured when they become nuisances around campgrounds and cabins. They're weighed, tattooed, measured, tagged, fitted with radio collars, and turned loose where we hunted sheep.

To make a very long story short, we had all sorts of fun dealing with griz when they came visiting at our camp. Fortunately we never had a confrontation, and I managed to take a nice ram on camera, which made the producers relieved and happy. We were also relieved and happy to pack up and get the heck out of there when the video production was completed.

The mule deer video was shot in Wyoming under the direction of Jerry Chiappetta, a well-known outdoor media person from Michigan. It took 28 days to do the tape, and we were bone-tired when it was finally completed.

Twice Jerry instructed me not to shoot when we had technical problems with gear or the light was wrong. Both times I had good muley bucks lined up in my sights, but I had to back off. I ended up taking a so-so buck, but we got the quick, humane kill shot that we wanted.

My elk videos were filmed in Idaho and Montana. The late-season elk production was filmed around Gardiner, Montana.

It was cold – real cold, like 20 below zero cold. There were times when we had to delay taping because I was half frozen to death and my teeth were chattering so bad I couldn't talk.

One afternoon, when cameraman Rick Morgan and I got back to town, we saw a couple bull elk standing in the street outside of a saloon, eating hay out of the bed of a pickup truck.

Rick and I decided to have some fun and shoot some footage. I walked between the bulls, tipped my hat and said "Howdy" to them, and entered the saloon.

Spencer Kaylor is a lucky boy. He got a dandy bull, and it was filmed on a video, too.

The shoot came out so well that the producer used it as a lead to the video. We couldn't have planned it any better.

Another time we were in deep snow, and I was tracking a bull, carrying my rifle with me. Finally, the camera shows me topping a ridge and looking down on a big six point bull. The camera switches back and forth between me and the bull, and finally, after the scene is built up with music and the audience is waiting for me to shoot, I smile into the camera, and say something like: "unfortunately I don't have an elk tag.........."

People who have seen the video tell me that when they watch that scene, they want to punch me in the nose. Just when they expect me to take the bull, I throw cold water on the scene. That's show business, though.

A youngster by the name of Spencer Kaylor saves the video. The 12-year-old shoots a dandy bull with a .308, and we got some good footage of the stalk, the kill, and some commentary afterward.

The elk bugling video was a major logistical effort. Rick Morgan and Producer/Director Ken Wilson followed me and outfitter Ken Smith around for days. It's a good thing Rick and Ken Wilson were in good physical condition, because they had to lug more than a hundred pounds of gear around in some of Idaho's nastiest cover.

Much of the video was a how-to production, showing me describing bugling techniques and other hunting requirements. The kill shot, however, absolutely amazed me.

Never in my life have I dropped a bull so hard as I did on-camera. Not only did he go down at my first shot, but he went down so hard that his chin cracked solidly on the ground and bounced back upwards.

It was the most humane shot I'd ever made, and I hadn't done anything differently than I ever had before. I was using Bertha, my well-worn .30/06 and simply managed to hit the bull's spinal column.

Again, that's show business, I suppose, but I'm for sure saying to heck with video productions.

(In the event you want to see my craziness on videos, you can rent them from most sporting goods stores. Or, you can order them from information provided at the back of this book).

Boots R. Reynolds

A lot has been said about Boots Reynolds, but most of it can't be printed. One printable comment was made, however, by a friend, who said, "He can buck a fella off harder with a paintbrush than any bronc I've ever seen!" Maybe that's because Boots has been down lookin' up enough times himself.

Boots is really Roy Reynolds, who was born and raised on the ranches of the Osage country of Oklahoma. It was on these ranches that he got his education as a cowboy. He's been on, over, under and around horses all his life and his career began at the age of eight as a brush track jockey riding matched races in Oklahoma.

Somehow in the early 70's Boots ended up in northern Idaho where he now resides with his wife, Becky, overlooking beautiful lake Pend Oreille near Sandpoint, Idaho, and where he devotes himself fulltime to drawing and painting.

Always seeing humor in his surroundings it was just a matter of time until his drawings became cartoons. After years of drawing these "funny pitchers" for friends and family he decided to try his hand at sharing them with the public. Somebody, somewhere, must have liked them as his pen and ink cartoons have appeared in such magazines as *Western Horseman, Horseman, ProRodeo Sports News, Horse and Horseman*, and *Horse and Rider*.

Somehow, despite the demand and popularity of his artwork, Boots has managed to find some spare pieces to hang in a few galleries. (Rumor has it that he pays them to hang his paintings.) He now has his work displayed in galleries in Issaquah, Washington, Coeur d'Alene, Idaho and Cody, Wyoming.

According to Boots, "I think the western art world and the public are ready for something a little different and the way things are going in the world we could all use a little more humor and I plan to give it to them. They can laugh at my stuff all they want to."

To order a print of the book cover and other humorous prints by Boots write for information and brochure to: R. Place, 195 Trestle Creek Rd., Hope, Idaho, 83836.

BOOKS and VIDEOS
by
JIM ZUMBO

BOOKS

All books will be autographed

TO HECK WITH ELK HUNTING – Jim's favorite hunting tales. Most are humorous, but some are bizarre. Illustrated by Boots Reynolds. $20.95 postpaid.

CALLING ALL ELK – The only book on the subject of elk hunting that covers every aspect of elk vocalization. $17.95 postpaid.

JIM ZUMBO'S GUIDE TO MODERN MULE DEER HUNTING – A jam-packed softcover that will lead you to big muleys. Foreward by Pat McManus. Lots of photos, tips, secrets, techniques, where-to, how-to. $11.95 postpaid.

HUNT ELK – The most comprehensive book ever written on elk hunting. This 260-page hardcover describes everything you've ever wanted to know about elk – bugling, hunting in timber, late season hunting, trophy hunting, solid advice on hunting on your own or with an outfitter, and lots more. $20.95 postpaid.

HUNTING AMERICA'S MULE DEER – The first book ever done on every phase of mule deer hunting. This thick 360-page hardcover is aclaimed to be the best on the subject. Plenty of photos, with valuable information on trophy hunting and where-to, and how-to hunt muley bucks. $22.95 postpaid.

HOW TO PLAN YOUR WESTERN BIG GAME HUNT – Are you dreaming of a western hunt? This softcover will start you in the right direction, with solid info on planning your hunt. Lots of maps and phone numbers, and precise info on all western big game species. $11.95 postpaid.

ALL AMERICAN DEER HUNTER'S GUIDE A big, 340 page hardcover with color photos that covers every aspect of hunting whitetails and muleys. Co-edited by Jim Zumbo and Robert Elman. Chapters by other experts such as Jim Carmichel, Craig Boddington, Erwin Bauer, Leonard Lee Rue, Byron Dalrymple, and many others. $32.95 postpaid.

VIDEOS

HUNTING BUGLING ELK WITH JIM ZUMBO – produced by Sportsmen On Film – 70 minutes. Watch Jim fly in to Idaho's Selway wilderness and hunt elk. This video is loaded with instructions and tips on elk bugling, and is climaxed by Jim taking a big 6-point bull on camera. $29.95 postpaid.

LATE SEASON ELK WITH JIM ZUMBO – produced by Sportsmen On Film – 38 minues. See huge elk plowing through deep powder snow, and watch a 12-year old boy take a big bull on camera. Lots of tips and techniques included. $29.95 post paid.

HUNTING AMERICA'S MULE DEER – produced by 3M Corp. – 60 minutes. Acclaimed to be the best mule deer video ever produced. Watch Jim stalk and kill a nice four-point buck. Plenty of specific info on techniques. Filmed in Wyoming. $24.95 postpaid.

HUNTING BIGHORN SHEEP WITH JIM ZUMBO – produced by Grunkmeyer Productions – 60 minutes. Watch Jim stalk and shoot a ram in Wyoming's spectacular Teton Wilderness with veteran outfitter Nate Vance. $52.95 postpaid.

AUDIO CASSETTES

E-Z ELK CALL INSTRUCTIONAL TAPE – 30 minutes. Jim Zumbo tells where, how and when to use the E-Z Elk Call, including hunt scenarios and situations. $12.95 postpaid.

HOW TO HUNT ELK IN CROWDED WOODS – 30 minutes. Jim explains how to beat the odds where competition from other hunters is heavy. $12.95 postpaid.

HOW AND WHERE TO HUNT TROPHY BULLS – Jim describes successful methods for hunting mature elk as well as specific where-to-go info in each elk state and Canadian province. 60 minutes. $15.95 postpaid.

E-Z ELK CALL

JIM ZUMBO'S E-Z ELK CALL – Made of very soft plastic, both calling edges are of different lengths, allow calls of varying pitches. $12.95 postpaid.

Order from

JIM ZUMBO
P.O. Box 2390
Cody, WY 82414

Check, money order or Visa/MC accepted. Credit card orders: please include number and expiration date. Allow 6 weeks for delivery. Canadian residents add $2.00 for each item for shipping.